M000197478

S. T. O. P
Start Thinking
Outside of Prison

Jermaine Ali Williams

Freebird Publishers
www.FreebirdPublishers.com

Freebird Publishers

Box 541, North Dighton, MA 02764
Info@FreebirdPublishers.com
www.FreebirdPublishers.com

Copyright © 2016
S.T.O.P. Start Thinking Outside of Prison
By Jermaine Ali Williams

All Freebird Publishers titles, imprints and distributed lines are available at special quantity discounts for bulk purchases for sales promotions, premiums, fundraising educational or institutional use.

ISBN: 0-9913591-4-3
ISBN-13: 978-0-9913591-4-1

Printed in the United States of America

Dedication

Dad a.k.a. The Champ and Mom, this book is for both of you. I will always love you and miss you dearly. You can now look down over your son and be proud. I won't let you down, whether incarcerated or as a free man. I will continue to be the man you always wanted me to be.

"God prepares great men for great tasks by great trials . . ."
J.K. Gressett

Contents

Acknowledgements

First, I want to thank the Most High for giving me the strength, courage, determination, and persistent nature to continue to endure my endeavors. My journey in life has led to the writing of this book. I want to thank my parents, Donnie and Wanda Williams-Lewis, for allowing me the blessing to inherit the genes of strong willed people. I love you both dearly.

I thank my Father, a Golden Gloves boxing award winner just like his father before him. Thank you for installing in me the instincts of a fighter. A quality I would need throughout my difficult birth and through the difficult hurdles and obstacles I would face in life.

I thank my Mother for allowing me the opportunity to see what a true woman represents. I have yet to find a better example in a woman than you. You are an example for all women to follow. I love you. I know it was hard raising a knucklehead like me. I truly apologize for any pain, agony, and discomfort I may have caused you.

I thank my siblings from the youngest up - my baby bro Mike, my right hand, my roaddog. If it wasn't for you, I don't know where I would be. You stood by me when I was at my lowest during the dark days. Through elementary, middle, to high school, then unfortunately through my incarceration.

I thank my sister Jamillah. You were there for me during my times of need. You supported and loved me with unconditional love.

I thank my oldest brother Reek. Your influence at times was good and bad, but having you as a brother helped shape me into the responsible man I am today. I'm proud of you and all that you've accomplished. I love you.

I thank my nephew Quan. I know I left the free world when you were just three years old. You probably have no idea how much I love you. I'm proud to see the young man you have grown to be.

I thank my nephew Nu-Nu. I came to prison in June of 2000; you were born that same year. Thus, we have spent very little time together in the free world. But I most certainly love you dearly.

I thank my nieces, my little ladies Diamond and Jamiyah. I met and watched both of you grow while you visited me behind these prison walls. It was not easy. Both of you deserved to have more. I should have been there, and I apologize for my unnecessary absence. I love both of you little angels.

I also want to thank my brothers and sisters-in-law.

I thank my friends who remained true during my times of adversity. You know who you are, but just to name a few - Dawon, Rissa, Lynn, John Doe, J-Ready, Cousin Rah (325), Rowdy Rah (Park St.), Will (325), Bart (The Ave), Karriem (Lil' Bricks), Dev (325), Roy Bryson (Big Unc), Kim Bryant, Saphia (Bradly Courts), Frenchie and Charmaine Jones (Chadwick Ave), Mega (9th Ave), Cookie, The Mayfields (108), Latrice Hinton (325), my Michigan fam- Dontay, Tiger, Nikki, Choya, Nicole Hunter, Latoya, Dawon, Derrick Byrd and Dawana.

I thank my grandparents, living and deceased (R.I.P.).

I thank my uncles and aunts, the living and deceased (R.I.P.). Aunt Pat, I love you beyond words.

I thank my cousins - Cora, Munch, James, Tish, Ricky, Peanut, Tasha, Eisha, Terri, Vee-Vee, Ro, Fred, Ernie, Mike, Tifa, Quita, Betty, Torian, Stasia, Hakeem, Sharik, Shaleek, Sharon, Kia, Sheeda, Ralph, Darnell, Tahshawn, Anita, Anthony, Kiana, Boot, Antwon, Jalisa, Jolette (R.I.P..), Danny (R.I.P..), Moo-Moo, Susan, Jenifer (R.I.P..), Naya, Fattie (R.I.P..), Hanif (Buck R.I.P..), Marlon, Joey, April (R.I.P..), Dave, Botch, Keisha, Davita, Noc (R.I.P..), Lil' Noc, Monte, Tiara, Ayeesha, Chrisi, Lil' Moo-Moo, Ebony, Tasha, Malisa, Jason, Fabian, Kia, and Meesa...too many to name...I love all of you including the ones I didn't mention.

R.I.P. to my comrades and fallen soldiers – Tez (325), Big-V (325), Lil' Will (108), Derrick (325), Colif (325), Mugsy (108), Speedy (The Ave.), Raven (325), Ronnie (The Ave.), Robbie (Park Ave.), Lil' Hass (325), Quinn aka Dawg (Park Ave.), Shaquita (R.I.P. my love), Lil Rah Rah (18th), Joe Clair (Springfield Ave.), and if there is anyone I forgot to mention, pardon my soul.

There are not very many, but thanks to the REAL MEN (they know who they are) locked down in Trenton State Prison and the rest of the institutions in Jersey. Stay strong! Hold ya head!

Lastly, I want to give a special thanks to all the haters, you know who you are. Thanks for the motivation. I could not have done it without you.

Introduction

Greatness lies within many of my brothers and sisters. The problem is we tend to find ourselves incarcerated before we discover this greatness. Our thought patterns and consistent inability to think on a positive level leads us straight to prison.

Too often, we conjure criminal suggestions to our lack of success. We scheme to sell drugs, commit robberies, burglaries, petty thefts, and other crimes - crimes that will eventually lead us to prison.

There is a hip hop artist who calls himself 50 Cent. He starred in a movie entitled *Get Rich or Die Trying* where he comments that, "if you add up all the time spent standing on a corner selling drugs, it is like earning minimum wage. Then, if you add up all the time likely to be spent in prison, it is even less than that." This is the true essence of thinking outside of prison; being able to evaluate the benefit and the consequence of our decision making.

During my incarceration, I have had the privilege of encountering some of the most talented and gifted people one could imagine. I never gained the full story behind each individual, but the same question would plague my mind with each encounter. With so many gifts, skills and talent, where did these people go wrong? Some had the artistic skills of Michelangelo. Some had the basketball talents of LeBron James. The boxing traits of Muhammad Ali. The lyrical artistry of Jay-Z. Again, where did these brothers go wrong? It was their thinking!

Thinking is very critical to one's success, failure, and survival. Every decision requires thinking. If not, many actions will be done on impulse. And impulsive behavior tends to bring about situations from which one needs to be rescued. Think of a preteen, teenager, or young adult, all of whom can possess the impulsive behaviors of children. If the impulses aren't tamed or controlled, the behavior patterns will be present in each stage of life. Maybe this is the reason I see so many 40-year-olds that lack self-control or the ability to deal with some of life's simplest problems. They can't attack the situations from a professional, calm, and diplomatic standpoint.

S.T.O.P. was written as a movement to help promote a greater thinking process - a thinking process I believe will slow down the recidivism rate within our communities. This will mean that more fathers will be available in the household, more parents around to pass down the guidance that will enable our young boys to become men. Men who will stand accountable for the direction of their community.

The black woman is a part of this cycle of pain, as well. Statistics say, for every thirty woman, there is only one black- man. Such a ratio undoubtedly leaves women with very few choices: single parents, lesbianism, bisexuality, or chasing after married men. These behaviors affect their emotional stability. The women are left angry, bitter, argumentative, frustrated, and confused. Even though they already know, they find themselves asking, Where are all the black men? Well, 2.5 million of them are in the U.S. penitentiary.

Through S.T.O.P., I want to develop a generation of great thinkers who will be able to side step prison altogether. This includes the people who already find themselves incarcerated. This movement is just beginning. It won't end with the completion of this book. Another goal is to produce a monthly magazine that will provide people with the latest insights on finances, health, technology, economics, the job market, and the benefits of being an American citizen. S.T.O.P. wants to provide community centers in the inner cities to help put the future of our children on the right track.

As a man, I ask all men to join together and help rebuild what many of us helped destroy. It starts with you. It starts with me. No outside force can aid this cause until the aid is given from within. A better future is literally in our hands. It is my intent that the following ten chapters will provide enlightenment and force all of us to S.T.O.P. - Start Thinking Outside Prison!

JERMAINE ALI WILLIAMS

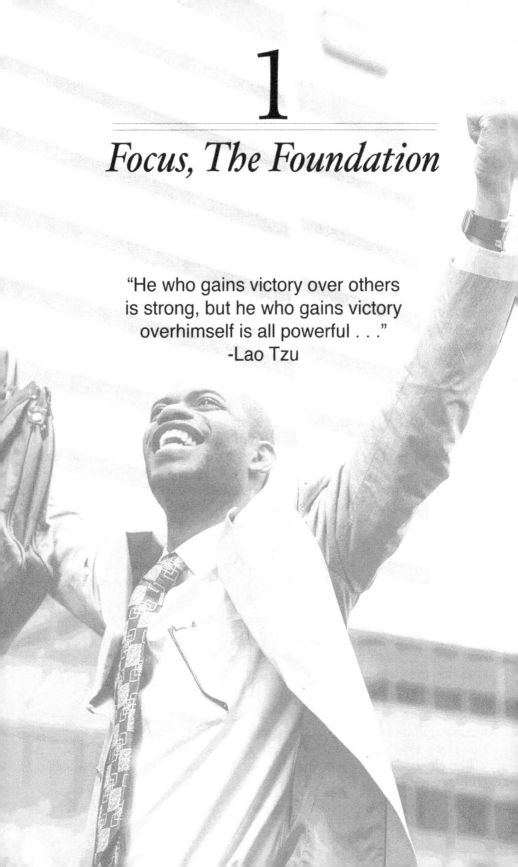

1

Focus, The Foundation

"He who gains victory over others
is strong, but he who gains victory
overhimself is all powerful . . ."
-Lao Tzu

Focus is a paramount place to begin. With so much going on at times, it can be hard to find focus. This is why I always try to maintain the qualities of being focused. There are five: determination, dedication, persistence, consistency, and patience.

Achieving a level of focus is key for one to Start Thinking Outside Prison. Before concentrating on the five qualities of focus, we first must determine if we have any focus at all. Denial is a problem in many lives; it was in mine, and it probably is in yours, too. Having the courage to admit I'm lost or to admit I don't have a solution to a problem in my life is not a thing that is easily done. Pretending to have priorities in order and actually having them in order are not the same thing. On top of that, we tend to not have the right attitude when attitude is everything! I'll use an example from one of my favorite movies, *South Central*. O.G. Bobby Johnson was continuously denied parole after serving 10 years. That shouldn't have come as a surprise to him because he had a few institutional infractions, along with an allegiance to the Deuce Gang. Then, a Muslim named Ali came along. He had been studying Bobby for some time, and had figured that Bobby's problem had everything to do with poor attitude.

Ali and Bobby Johnson began conversing. Ali fed him books and lectured him on his moral conduct. Shortly after, Bobby removed the purple heart from beneath his eye (the heart was a stain of honor symbolizing a murder Bobby had committed). O.G. Bobby cut his braids off and took on a more presentable look. And finally, the subject of parole had come up again. Bobby told Ali that he had been denied numerous times. To that, Ali spoke one simple word… attitude. He told Bobby that his attitude must speak that he was a changed man. He told him his attitude needed to reflect his thoughts. Bobby's reward for changing his appearance and attitude was parole.

He needed to get out of his own way. He needed to realize that a poor attitude yielded poor results. How he spoke to people and conducted himself took him further than he could imagine.

I learned a great deal from that movie. Adversity breeds character. So I don't let life's experiences shape my character for the worst. I let the hate, pain, and rejection motivate every bone in my body. People are going to hate me, they are going to hate you, for no particular reason. That's their problem, not ours.

Adopt Obama's policy of "Forward!" In life we are going to experience enormous amounts of pain from death, failed relationships, and other setbacks. Don't let it slow you down. Again, adopt Obama's policy. All sorts of doors will be closed in your face. But stay persistent and keep knocking until opportunity answers.

We've already mentioned determination, which involves an astute will power. You must determine to not go back to prison. You must determine to do what is necessary to be well accomplished. You must determine to master the man or woman that has been holding you down for so long. You must determine to struggle through the peer pressure, distractions, and temptations of the outside world. You must determine to start and finish each goal you set. Determination is about having your mind made up, knowing in which direction you want your life to go. Even in the face of failure, determination must continue to be in the forefront.

Let's look at Russell Simmons. If it weren't for his determination, Phat Farm clothing line would have never prevailed. Russell ventured off into the fashion business with a partner, launching the line Phat Farm. After millions were invested into marketing, Russell and his business partner realized that the investment was not beneficial. The loss was tremendously greater than the gain. Russell's partner even withdrew his share before Phat Farm was able to get off the ground. He eventually opted out of the investment altogether.

Russell, however, was determined. After modeling and marketing Phat Farm in Europe and all over the world, Russell observed the sales pick up, and Phat Farm began to rise. Russell, now the sole owner of Phat Farm, received 100% of the revenue. It was his determination that kept him moving the project forward, even after his associate had bailed out.

Phat Farm became a national and international success even further expanding into Baby Phat. If Russell would have bailed out along with his prior business partner, he would have never known Phat Farm's full potential. Russell didn't let his competition slow him down or the business world shut him out. He was determined to make Phat Farm a success. Didn't consider failure an option. Be determined like Russell was to win at all costs.

Dedication is a very important pillar of the focus foundation. With no dedication, you'll find yourself running in place, getting nowhere fast.

Coming home from prison isn't easy. Trying to become financially stable while readjusting to society will take dedication. Unfortunately, you may need to start from the bottom up to get to where you want to be. The only way you can climb a ladder is from the bottom up. There will be no Jiffy Pop microwave success.

It's imperative that you hit the ground running, considering how much time you spent incarcerated. Understand success won't come over night. But it's the dedication that you put into your journey toward prosperity that will produce prosperous fruit.

Success has three levels. In order to gain ideal economic wealth, you must dedicate time and focus toward figuring out what level you are on. You take in what you put out. You may want to ask yourself - do I have any skills? Do I have a high school diploma? Who will hire me? Starting to think outside prison is going to be hard for most. Especially when you are used to utilizing your thoughts for criminal activities. For the ones who have not been to prison, you have a slight advantage. Without a felony, you will still qualify for county, state, and federal jobs. In addition, the benefits of the U.S. military. Take advantage! You can beat the odds.

The rest of us, my advice is to first take the initiative to achieve the small goals. If you don't have a high school diploma or a G.E.D., get one! If you don't have a skill or trade, get one! Being certified in a specific area will land you job security. Be dedicated to gaining these basic requirements of the job force. The significance of a college degree will be discussed later in the book.

Every morning you must wake up and search the classified section of the newspaper for job openings. "Help Wanted" is posted throughout the section. You may need to start on a minimum wage level just to get the ball rolling a bit. Dedicate yourself to your minimum wage job and stack your dollars.

After you get into a suitable routine, then you can sign up for a trade course during your off hours - this can even be done on line. Remember, dedication and hard work. Set a two- year goal for yourself of straight grinding. Live by the popular urban mantra, "If you grind hard, you shine hard." But don't let the grinding distract you from proper budgeting - another topic which will be discussed later.

The same energy we used to put into selling drugs is the exact same energy required to start thinking outside prison. That means finding two minimum-wage jobs if you have to. The plan is to work 16-hour weekdays for 24 months. That should earn you an average of $500 dollars every two weeks from each job. That's $1,000 every two weeks and $2,000 every month.

A prisoner somehow manages to live off - on average - $15 to $85 per month. There are no bills in prison, but many costs have to be incurred by the prisoner his or herself. The money comes and goes, it's no different than the outside world. The bottom line is it will take discipline with dedication and no deviation.

Make the 24-month goal your motivation. And be sure to stay on point with minimizing your spending. $2,000 a month for a person with no obligations, other than to care for himself, is a great starting point. Easily, $1,000 per month could be put away in savings. With a precise budgeting plan, you can very well be on your way to financial stability. In 24 months, with diligence, you can save $24,000 dollars!

Nonetheless, your living quarters should fit your budget. A one-bedroom or a studio apartment should suffice. Shop around for the lowest costs ($500-$600 dollar range). You will rarely be home during these first two years, so your utility bills should be low. $300-$400 dollars a month can be set aside for food, clothing, and cosmetics. Often times, you will be wearing your work uniform, which reduces your clothing costs. Lastly, $100 should be put aside for transportation.

That's a $1,000 budget plan for 24 months. If you dedicate yourself, you'll be ready for the next stage of finance, investments, which is learning how to make your money make money. Again, to be discussed later.

The third pillar of your focus foundation is persistence. Persistence equals will power, ambition, and resilience. To truly start thinking outside prison, your approach needs to be one of persistence. Do not be seduced into turning back to your old ways. The struggle will be intense at times. Remember, it's not about how you fall, but how you get back up. Or another popular quote, "It's not about how you start the race, it's how you finish." The obstacles will be there; some will be put there intentionally. But your desire for your goals must be kept strong. When one door closes, knock on the next one. It is easier to give in when the pressure is too thick, but the one who fights against the current will develop a tenacious attitude towards life. No matter what, you must believe in what you are doing and move forward in an ambitious, resilient manner.

Not many things in this world can take the place of persistence. Talent can't take its place. And there are so many unsuccessful men whom possess talent. Genius can't take its place either. Unrewarded genius is almost a proverb. Education certainly can't take the place of persistence. The world is filled with educated derelicts.

Pressing on can be the solution to all of your problems. When you are fired from your job, press on! When adversity hits your doorstep, press on! Like it is mentioned earlier, keep moving forward. You can't look back on life with regrets. There is no going back in time, so don't even look back. The future is for you to shape and mold to your desire. Take full control of your life.

And this leads us to the 4th pillar of our focus foundation, consistency. Be consistent with putting action behind your thoughts. Action and consistency go hand-and-hand. Yet we sometimes fall short on being repetitious. Establishing a routine and following through with it is key. Learn to start things, then finish them. That is the only way you will be able to reap the reward of consistency. Getting up every morning and doing the same routine - going to work, school, and only sleeping when you are truly tired. This notion may seem boring, but it's the long term that you must be concerned with. If you stay consistent with your goals, at the end of it all, you will appreciate what you have earned. In addition to that, you will have obtained a sense of achievement of which you can be proud.

Consistency always comes with reward. If you exercise regularly, the reward will be a fit physique. Put the same attitude towards thinking outside prison. Your life will have no choice but to change for the better.

The last pillar of your focus foundation will bring your focus full circle - patience! "A man's wisdom gives him patience," Proverbs 19:11. Considering this passage from the Bible, it is fair to say that a patient man is a wise man. Things that are rushed are often not produced in its finest quality.

It won't be easy giving up tax-free money, having your own set hours, living lavishly. These are all descriptions of a drug dealers lifestyle. Now, you will have to pay taxes. You will have to fix a budget. And, most important, work hard for everything you own. Working hard for a thing makes it difficult for that thing to be taken from you.

The down side to selling drugs is that your whole life can be stripped from you in one raid. But the one who goes to work and earns what is his has displayed self-control and discipline. I speak from experience because, indeed, I am an ex-drug dealer. I had all the glitz and glamour, especially the nice car. What's crazy is that my cousin, who went to trade school, was driving around in a car just like mine! I used to be out there risking my life! Running from the stick-up boys. Dodging the cops. Yet, my cousin had what I had, and he didn't have to dodge any bullets to get it! In fact, to this day, my cousin owns a house, he's married, and he's driving a car more expensive than anything I've ever owned!

My lack of patience, self-control, and self-discipline has left me confined to a jail cell for over a decade. Remember, the greatest asset we have is time, whether we have a little or a lot. Patience is about managing your time and energy. Everything will happen within the fullness of time. Start thinking outside prison. Practice the pillars of the focus foundation to perfection. You may fail from time to time. But know that failure presents the greatest opportunity to learn who you really are. Adversity is like patience; it reveals your strengths by enhancing your thinking ability. Thus, it forces you to channel your focus. So, S.T.O.P. (Start Thinking Outside Prison), and focus.

2

Life Skills, Part 1

"Poverty sits by the cradle of all our great
men, and rocks all of them to manhood . . ."
- Heinrich Heine (1797-1856)

Escaping poverty isn't easy. But it is twice as hard without the life skills for re-adjusting to society. It begins with having an agenda. The agenda must have purpose. And the purpose must entail priorities. To start thinking outside prison, you will need to acquire some necessary life skills, being crippled by lack of knowledge plagues the inner city. "If you knew better, you would do better." And knowing better means acquiring life skills.

Let's start with budgeting. It should not have to be explained why setting financial goals is important. Part of those financial goals is to prepare a personal budget and keep records. This is not a fantasy world. Real life requires preparation. In California, a television commercial sponsored by the state lottery showed a young man pushing a cart down the aisle in a home-supply-warehouse store. This man looked down a row of power tools and announced to the clerk, "I'll take all of these."

Unfortunately, most of us have a better chance of being struck by lightning then we have of winning the lottery. Some of us tend to live inside a financial fantasy world. Some people spend money as if they have unlimited resources. I'm sure you know someone like this. Wise consumers, on the other hand, live in a real world. They work hard and know exactly what their financial obligations are. They are responsible people and live within their means. In the long run, these people not only sleep better, but they also enjoy life better.

The main tool of the smart consumer is a budget. A budget is an organized plan for spending money. According to this plan, a person matches their spendable income to their expected outflow. This process will help provide for immediate needs, future needs, and will also remove the need for borrowing money just to meet normal living expenses. And, if you establish a realistic budget and use it as a financial guide, prudent planning will afford you more of the things you need and want.

Disposable income is another term for spendable income. This is money that one can spend within their means on virtually anything they want. Working 40 hours a week for $8.00 per hour will give a person a gross income of $320. Federal, State, and Social Security withholding taxes and voluntary deductions will lessen that gross income by an average of 25%. So, the actual take-home pay is around $240. This is your disposable income.

Now that we've determined our disposable income, we can explore some of the many ways of budgeting to discover which budget plan works best for us. Let's look at seven specific steps.

STEP 1: DETERMINE YOUR BUDGET GOALS

Budgeting your disposable income begins with setting some practical goals. Whatever you are trying to achieve should be realistically doable. Every objective should be geared toward itemizing your budget process. Prioritize and write down any goal that will require spending money. Once this is done, we can move on to the next budgeting stage.

STEP 2: TRY TO DETERMINE YOUR EXPECTED INCOME

Let's say you have a full-time job that pays a total of $17,000 per year. Based on an average of 25% withholding tax, your weekly net income would be reduced to $245.19, which makes your monthly income $1,062.50. This would be your disposable or spendable income - the amount of money you can realistically expect to take home. Your budget and goals will be put to the reality test through your monthly expenses.

STEP 3: DETERMINE YOUR EXPENSES

There are two types of expenses: fixed expenses and variable expenses. Fixed expenses are those that are major expenses. Such as rent mortgage, car payments, insurance premiums, utilities and other things of the like. Some fixed expenses are due monthly. Others may be due quarterly or semi-annually. This is often true of insurance premiums - the amount paid to an insurance company for the protection your policy provides. The most common types of insurance are automobile insurance, life insurance, health insurance, and personal property insurance. There is also renter's insurance.

Variable expenses are those that might change according to your needs. They are based on short-term goals that are subject to change during the year. Entertainment, clothing, personal needs, cosmetics, and many household items are some of the things listed under this category.

A few dollars should also be put away each pay period to build up a savings account. Perhaps you have something specific you wish to buy; a savings account will aid you in this without cutting into other expenses. Or you could just be preparing for that proverbial rainy day. Rainy days, unfortunately, have expenses that will sneak up on us.

Generally, financial advisors say that most people can save only about 100% of their disposal income. That means $10 out of every $100. It's always possible to put aside more than that. But doing so might require additional sacrifice, belt tightening as it is commonly called. What does this mean? It means wearing no-name brands instead of Timberland or Gucci boots. Instead of a car that requires a payment of $600 a month, settle for a cheaper used car that may cost you $3,000 in total.

There will always be minor variable expenses. They are usually the habits you create that do not fit neatly into any category. These expenses can be listed as miscellaneous in your budget. Between your fixed and variable expenses, you can expect to come up with a list of budget items that look something like the following:

Housing	Transportation
Household Items	Utilities
Medical Expenses	Insurance
Food	Entertainment
Savings	Miscellaneous
Clothing	Personal Needs

If your utilities are included in your rent, then you can omit this expense from your budget.

To start thinking outside prison, you must learn the value of a dollar. Budgeting money properly will help. So will knowing how to manage a household. Many households have failed marriages and are possibly dysfunctional due to mismanagement. But most, if not all, of these households could have been saved if the head of the house would have put the needs before the wants. This is what it means to start thinking outside prison.

STEP 4: MAKE A BUDGET WORK SHEET

Preparation is key in any endeavor. The easiest way to start preparing a budget is to study your current expenses. If you have a checking account, look into your check register for the past couple of months. Where does your disposable money go? If most of your purchases are made with cash, look for old receipts you have kept. Or try to recall what you purchased and how much you have spent. Learn to keep control of what you are earning and spending.

STEP 5: TRY IT OUT FOR A WHILE

You won't have to keep an itemized record of your expenditures forever, just long enough to see the pattern of where your money is going. One way to track your expenses is to make a set of index cards and label one card for each of your budget items. Write the month and year on the card. Start a new set of cards at the beginning of each month. Keep these cards in an envelope marked Budget Cards. Indicate the month and year on this envelope, also. Every time you pay for something, keep the receipt. When you get home, write the date, the item you purchased, and the cost on the appropriate index card. Doing this will help you keep a good record of how you are spending your money. It will tell you whether or not you are sticking to your budget. Be sure to keep your monthly envelopes and index cards for the whole year. You will need them in December when it is time to map out your budget for the upcoming year.

Budgeting for the next year is actually easier than creating your first budget. The reason is you already have a track record of steady income, which you have already been monitoring. One of the first things to consider is whether you expect any changes in your income. Will it remain the same? Will it go up? Or even decrease? All of these things need to be considered in your disposable income, beginning the month after your income has changed.

Some people receive a payment known as a yearly living adjustment cost. This raise is linked to the national inflation rate. The inflation rate is the average rise in consumer prices for all classes of goods and services. The more money, the more problems.

STEP 6: STAY CONSISTENT WITH YOUR BUDGET

Once you have a fairly stable budget that works, you need to stick with it. Your budget is a beacon that will help keep you financially stable. It should give you the feeling that you are in control of your life. Without a budget, you could soon find your bills are out of control. Allowing that to happen can have negative results, which in turn could affect your decision making.

STEP 7: PRIORITIZE YOUR LIFE

When designing your budget, it is important to establish your priorities. You must decide what things are really needed when putting away money for living expenses. Essentials, of course, are food, shelter, clothing, and utilities. Then come other expenses such as transportation, personal needs, and household items. Unfortunately, that dream vacation to Brazil is a low-level priority. It's something to plan, but only after all the important matters of your budget have been secured.

It's easier to spend the money than to earn the money. This is why the wise consumer sets a realistic, practical budget and lives by it. If you follow these seven steps, you too will be one of those wise consumers. Your chances of increasing your financial status will greatly improve. And you may even start to increase your savings little by little.

The street life doesn't come with structure, order, or management. The terminology I frequently hear is "ballin' out" or "makin[1] it rain." "Ballin' out" or "makin' it rain" contributes to why most people come to prison! Many crimes are motivated by money. The street life will urge you to earn your money illegally instead of searching for a steady job.

It is hilarious how the hardest thugs won't work at Burger King or McDonalds, but they will go to prison and work eight hours a day for two dollars a day! Prisoners are forced to stick to their budget plans, which is about $60 a month on average. My message is . . . why wait until you go to prison? The same thing can be done in the free world. It may take you a little longer to get what you want and where you want to be, but the bottom line is you won't be going to prison just to learn how to budget your money.

Life skills start at home during your adolescence years. What you learn during those impressionable times tend to stick with you into adulthood. Often, this time determines how responsible or irresponsible you will be. You can change the cycle. Your past doesn't need to be your future. You can take control of your life, manage your life, and S.T.O.P. - Start Thinking Outside Prison!

3

Life Skills, Part 2

"Success is a great deodorant. It takes
away all your past smells . . ."
-Elizabeth Taylor

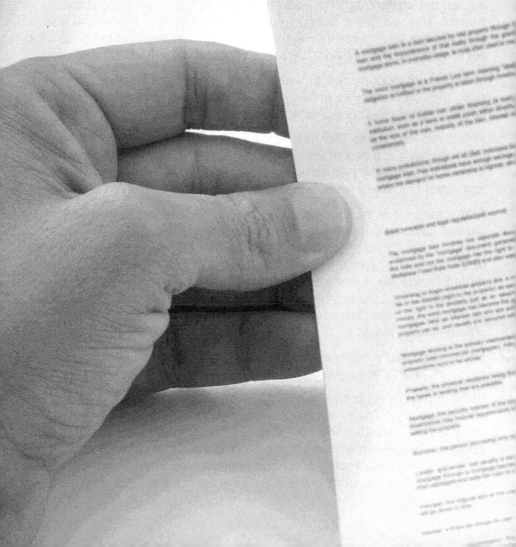

With success comes securing your wealth: making wise decisions about health, life, auto, and home insurance. Knowing how to secure your life and wealth is not only important to you, but to your family as well.

A funeral could be costly if you leave this world unexpectedly while not having your life insured. Or disaster may strike your possessions that are also uninsured. This can force immediate hardship upon your loved ones. Securing yourself is crucial to your willingness to start thinking outside prison.

Living day to day or paycheck to paycheck can be stressful. Everything you love and own can be swept from under you in the blink of any eye. Here, we will explore the many ways to secure yourself and the ones you love.

It is easy to understand the importance of putting money aside to purchase something like a car or a home. Other things we buy are not so easy to understand or explain. A good example is insurance. Insurance is an agreement or contract that you enter into with an insurance company or insurer. This company will pay your bills if you suffer a financial loss. In fact, you are buying something that does not even exist yet because it has yet to happen. It might only happen sometime in the future.

In order to collect from the insurance company, you have to become ill, need medical care, die, wreck your car, have it stolen or have something terrible happen to your home or personal property.

In our modern world, the need for insurance against the most common financial risks is a fact of life. Every consumer who wants to be a conscientious, responsible person recognizes the need for protection against the four kinds of losses mentioned above.

Auto insurance is so important to the whole society that many states have passed laws making it illegal to operate a motor vehicle without being insured. A driver's license or insurance was never a concern during my years of lawless living. This may sound like some of you, but I used to have no regard for the law. I was selling drugs, getting money, smoking weed, and nobody could tell me anything. My car had the temporary tag in the window, and I had no intention of getting it registered. No registration meant no official license plate.

Nonsense! This immature way of thinking is neither you nor me anymore! S.T.O.P., Start Thinking Outside Prison!

Returning to being properly insured - The written contract you make with an insurance company is called a policy. The payments you make to the company are called premiums. You, the policyholder, are also called the insured. The person who is licensed to sell insurance policies is an insurance agent or insurance broker. The financial value of the items you wish to insure is your insurable interest. And the service the insurance company provides for you is simply called coverage.

When a loss occurs, the insured must submit a claim. Actual payments for losses are called benefits. These basic terms apply to all types of insurance programs. The most basic insurance plans can be purchased separately or in combination within a single policy.

Here are some of these types of insurance. Hospital and surgical insurance is designed to pay all or part of the insured hospital bills, surgeon fees, and any miscellaneous charges connected to a hospital stay. Medical expense insurance covers routine office visits to your doctor that are not connected to a stay in the hospital.

Major medical insurance is intended to cover the medical services that go beyond the basic coverage of a hospital, surgical, or medical expense policy. It covers serious and costly rehabilitation treatment, such as physical therapy following a stroke or recovery time after sustaining an injury.

Disability insurance coverage helps those who are self- employed to replace lost income when illness or injury keeps them from earning a living for a prolonged period.

Other things that fall under health care coverage are prescription drugs, dental insurance, and eye care. You can purchase these privately. Most employers today choose to purchase prepaid health plans for their workers. They purchase these health plans from health care providers. The members or subscribers to these health plans receive health care from member physicians.

Currently, prepaid plans fall into three basic categories: (1) Health Maintenance Organizations. These organizations emphasize preventive medical care. The idea is to keep their members healthy so they will not need expensive hospital care. All members must go to a central facility for treatment. They may or may not be able to choose their physicians or see the same physician each time. (2) Preferred Provider Organizations. It is becoming increasingly common for doctors and hospitals to contract with businesses to provide medical services to their employees for a fixed price. (3) Individual Practice Associations. In this type of structure, patients covered by the I.P.A. insurance must choose from a list of member physicians who have agreed to treat the plans subscriber. The doctors may also see non I.P.A. patients. When a specialist is needed, subscribers must be referred by their primary care physician and must choose among those on an I.P.A. approved list.

Moving on to life insurance. One of the last things a young adult wants to think about is dying. The vast majority of twenty-something year old will live another 50 years, at least. They are getting educations, entering the work force, marrying, and having babies. All of their emphasis is on living.

The thought of planning for death seems depressing. Still, it is important to consider the real fact that death can occur at any time. However, living life today and planning for your future should be your primary concern. It is an act of maturity and responsibility to at least learn about life insurance. Also to determine whether you owe it to those you love to have this type of insurance.

Life insurance is like health insurance to a degree. It is a contracted agreement that you make with an insurance company upon which you must make payments. The company in turn agrees to pay a certain amount of money to the person you elect as your beneficiary.

How much life insurance do you need? This question has been approached in many ways. Getting a clear and simple answer can sometimes be difficult. The easiest answer is most married people need to be insured for about five times their net pay. Especially if they have children. Suppose your gross $20,000 annually. Your net pay is 75% of that, roughly $15,000. Financial experts would advise you to insure your life for about $75,000. If you were to die, your spouse and children would have a better chance adjusting to loosing you without having to adopt a lower standard of living.

The two broad categories of life insurance are term life insurance and cash value life insurance. Within each of these categories there are a variety of options. The key to term life insurance is that you are buying only one thing with your premium dollars; a certain amount of money payable in the event of your death. This payout is called the policies death benefit or simply its face amount. The person you name to receive the death benefit is your beneficiary. One of the chief advantages of term insurance is the relatively low premiums. Especially for people just entering adulthood. A disadvantage of term insurance is that the premiums continue going up as you get older.

The most common type of term life insurance is annually or yearly renewable term insurance. This type of policy expires yearly on the anniversary date, as long as the premiums have been paid. This policy is guaranteed renewable. Each year, the premium will raise slightly on a prearranged scale.

Cash value insurance differs from term insurance. In addition, to buying a death benefit, you are using your insurance policy to build a cash account. Your premium is higher than term premiums because of the cash building element. However, your premiums are likely to stay the same throughout the duration of the policy. As with term insurance, there are different forms of cash value insurance.

Whole life insurance is also called straight life and ordinary life insurance. Your policy is designed to build cash slowly. If you are still alive at the age of 100, the cash in the policy will equal the face amount. For example, suppose you purchased a $100,000 policy at age 35. You live to celebrate your 100th birthday. First, your premiums must have been paid the entire time. The policy will expire on the policy anniversary date during that year and the insurance company will send you a check for $100,000.

It is best for a young family to have some life insurance than none at all. Most experts would advise you to buy term insurance first with death benefits that you can afford. As income increases, then you may choose to switch to cash value life insurance.

Many of the insurance companies offer convertible term policies. This means that the policyholder has the option to convert the term insurance to a cash value policy at any time or at certain stated intervals.

If you cannot afford to purchase a life insurance policy equal to five times your take home pay, buy the most insurance you can afford. You can always build on that foundation later. There are other insurance programs you can apply for when you are out of work and the future does not look so bright. Before you decide to return to a life of crime, let's explore the options you will also need to start thinking outside prison.

Social Security Insurance. The U.S. congress passed the Social Security Act in 1935. In part, this legislation was a response to the wide-spread poverty created by the Great Depression of the 1930's. The initial goal of the program was rather simple, an established national fund to help unemployed retired workers and their dependents. The money for the fund was generated by mandatory contributions from both employers and employees. In the industries covered by the act, the main provisions of the Social Security Act are retirement income, disability insurance, unemployment insurance, survivors insurance, and health insurance.

One thing to keep in mind is that although social security is a treasured American benefit program, changes in the law are occurring and will surely continue to occur. It has been increasingly difficult to fund all the programs currently included in the law. You owe it to yourself as a worker and U.S. citizen to stay well-informed about the law and any proposed changes.

Retirement income. The law never intended to provide a full living for retired workers. Rather, the idea was to supplement the savings that people had put aside all their lives for their post-employment years. It is extremely difficult to maintain a desirable standard of living on social security benefits alone. If you are required by law to pay into the system, most workers now are, the amount you receive when you retire is based on the level of your earnings. Especially later in their careers than they do in the beginning. The system is geared to pay maximum benefits if you retire at the age of 65.

A worker can retire and draw reduced benefits as early as age 62. Changes in the law raised the retirement age to 67 in 2000. We can certainly expect more changes. The law places a limit upon how much a retiree can earn up to age 70 while still receiving benefits. Once wages pass that limit, the retiree is penalized by a reduction of his or her social security benefits. The law allows seniors age 70 or older to earn an unlimited amount without losing benefits.

The original social security law requires each state to operate a program providing income for temporarily unemployed workers. The funding for this program comes from an employer's state tax. Not from the wages of the employees. To be eligible, an unemployed worker must have held a job covered by the unemployment legislation for a minimum length of time. The worker must be laid off from the job and not fired. To receive benefits, the worker must register at the state office of unemployment and file a formal claim. He or she must also be available and willing to work if offered a job with a new employer.

In the future, the Social Security Act could be seeing reforms in the health insurance branch due to Obamacare. In 1965, congress added two programs to the Social Security Act that have become household names in every inner-city home across America - Medicare and Medicaid. These programs are funded by taxpayer dollars in the form of joint contributions by the federal and state governments. Basically, Medicare provides health insurance for people over 65. Millions of workers in America are covered by employer-sponsored health insurance. Not many companies are willing to fund lifelong health insurance for their retirees anymore. That is why Medicaid has become so important.

Medicaid provides medical care for the indigent of any age. Medicare and Medicaid are important programs that will affect you directly. First as a taxpayer, and at some point in time, as one who receives benefits. Both programs are undergoing a great deal of restructuring. Changes are certain to occur throughout your lifetime. As a good citizen and smart consumer of health services, you owe it to yourself and your family to be knowledgeable about the current status of these programs.

My parents, and probably yours, were thinking outside prison because I am a recipient of Medicaid. I remember when I was little, I didn't understand much then, but my mother used to give me a Medicaid card when it was time for me to go to the doctor for anything.

There are a few more important facts about social security you should know. The Internal Revenue Service, which collects taxes for the federal government, uses your social security number as your taxpayer identification number. This number is required on all your tax forms and tax payments. To qualify for social security, you must pay into the system for 10 or more years. That amounts to a minimum of 40 quarters (90-day periods).

If you have children and will claim them as dependents on your annual tax returns, you must apply for a social security card for each of them, granted they are at least one year old.

There is absolutely no retirement plan in the streets! Or prison for that matter. Too many souls return to the earth foolishly and unprepared due to a lack of knowledge and life skills required to prevail and survive. This is largely due to parents and guardians who lack the skills themselves to teach the child necessary tools for survival. They were probably never taught themselves because they were babies having babies.

A lion doesn't abandon its cubs in the wild without teaching them the necessary skills to survive. The same rule applies for humans. We must be properly prepared for life's pits and traps. This is one reason why so many of us end up in prison. We typically leave the nest unprepared.

1 in 4 African Americans are poor. 15% earn less than $15,000 a year, and 12% live below the poverty line. According to the U.S. Census Bureau, U.S. poverty is compared to Bulgaria and Yugoslavia - two places where poverty is wide-spreading. Without strong wings, we cannot soar and fly. An eagle doesn't guide its newborns out of the nest until they are ready to fly. Get under the guardians in your family. Listen and learn the keys of life, so you can contribute to society in a more productive way, securing yourself for the long haul. S.T.O.P. (Start Thinking Outside Prison) and learn the many avenues and skills of life.

4

Life Skills, Part 3

"Nothing in all the world is more dangerous than
sincere ignorance and conscientious stupidity . . ."
- Martin Luther King Jr.

There is so much that I learned about having a car. Growing up in the cities of Orange and Newark, New Jersey, it was common to hear stolen cars zipping up and down the avenues all night long. I didn't understand the value of the car nor the jeopardy of not having one. I remember owning several cars. Never once taking the responsibility to get a license, registration, or insurance. "Catch me if you can!" That's how I played with the police. The result of that was having plenty of vehicles confiscated. This was a waste of money on each occasion.

There are rules and regulations to owning and operating a vehicle. In order to start thinking outside prison, you must learn every aspect of your duties as an adult. Some of us had criminals in our families or even as parents, so we never got to experience the ins and outs, do's and don'ts of life. We picked up a criminal mindset from our families and friends.

There is a right way to live our lives, and we must learn that life has so much more to offer. Living the right way means having proper insurance for our automobiles - at least the minimum coverage. A driver can be cited for operating an uninsured vehicle on public roads. What we tend to forget is that an automobile traveling at even minimal speeds is a deadly weapon. If abused, it can cause great loss to life and property.

Also, the cost of buying a new car is rising steadily. This rise is also reflected in the increasing value of older, used cars. As a result, even a simple fender-bender can create costly damages. If an injury results from an accident, medical bills can rapidly skyrocket. Society has rightly decided that innocent victims of automobile accidents should not have to pay the cost of medical care for their injuries or repairs to their vehicles and other personal property. Responsible drivers recognize this.

The best way to assure safety is to drive safely at all times. Most importantly, be sure to carry adequate insurance on all of your motor vehicles.

The cost of auto insurance can be hard to predict. It is possible that you and your neighbor could have the exact same make and model car, but your insurance premiums can differ severely. Determining factors include the community in which you reside, your age, sex, and marital status. This is how a person's driver classification is determined. Your past and present driving record will also be considered, along with the year, make and, model of your car. All of these things will impact your limits of protection - however much you can pay out of your pocket before an insurance company takes over payment of the bills - simply put, your deductibles.

The last factor is how many times in the past you have filed a claim with the insurance company to be paid for automobile related damages. This is called your claims history. Now it is perceivable how you and your neighbor might not pay the same premiums even though you are driving identical cars.

Insurance companies do not mean cities as a whole when they speak of communities. They look at the histories of neighborhoods by breaking down the entire map into sections called rating territories. Your premiums can be different depending upon the part of the city in which you live. Insurance companies keep track of every accident and claim. They know from experience that if you live in a certain part of the city opposed to another, you are more likely to be involved in an accident.

Those who live in the most rural areas of the United States are most likely to pay the lowest premiums based on the community factor. Those of us living in the inner cities tend to pay more than the people in the suburbs.

Rating territory is only one of the premium setting factors. Another factor, driver classification, has become a controversial issue over the years according to claims statistics. Auto insurers have, for many years, charged higher premiums for younger male drivers than females. Sensitive to sex discrimination issues, states have begun to prohibit sex as a factor. However, single drivers tend to have more accidents than married drivers. Therefore, insurers will factor your marital status into your rates. And, it goes without saying, that older drivers have a better safety record than younger drivers.

A person's driving record is another factor. How many traffic citations do you have on your record? Moving violations, not parking tickets, enter into the rate decision. To a lesser degree, insurance companies consider how many miles you drive to and from work or school. Then the amount of miles you drive in a year. Insurers also wish to know if you use your vehicle for business or for pleasure. These sorts of questions are asked of you directly on most insurance applications.

The applications also ask you for the year, make, and model of your car. This is because auto insurers know the value of every car. They know exactly what it should cost to repair every piece and every part of every car. It is their business to know these things because they cannot afford to overpay for repairs and replacements of an insured automobile. As a result, an older car costs less to insure than a hot, new model you just drove off the lot.

Before purchasing a car, especially a new one, check with an insurance agent about the cost of insurance. Insuring a sedan is not at all the same thing as insuring a convertible. This is important because you may be able to afford the car payment but not the insurance premiums.

Deductibles are also considered. A general principle for purchasing any type of insurance is to determine how much you can pay out of your own pocket. What should be insured is every single loss that exceeds that amount. How much can you afford to pay if you are ever injured or if your car is ever damaged? Perhaps nothing! If so, you need a no-deductible policy, which will carry the highest premium. Maybe you can afford to pay a few hundred to a thousand dollars. Maybe more. In that case, your premium will be lower because the insurance company's risk will be reduced.

Another thing to consider is the limits of protection. The basic amount of insurance protection a driver must have is often set by law. You are, however, advised to carry as much insurance as you can afford. A single auto accident with multiple bodily injuries can result in damages amounting to millions.

Your responsibility for damages resulting from the operation of your car is called liability. There are two types of auto related liabilities, which were mentioned earlier - property damage liability and bodily injury liability. When purchasing auto insurance, you are making a contract with the insurer. The insurer agrees to pay the cost of damages you cause to the property of other people. You are also liable for a person's bodily damages. After you pay the deductible amount, the company will pay up to the dollar limit of the insurance you have purchased. Beyond that limit, the obligation of payment comes back to you.

Insurance limits are structured in two ways - single limit and split limit. Single limit coverage is a lump sum amount that the company will pay for a single accident. Suppose you purchase $100,000 of single limit coverage, then you cause an accident. It doesn't matter how many people are injured as a result of that accident; the insurance company will cover the cost up to $100,000.

Split limit coverage works differently. Your liability coverage may be structured on the basis of 50/100/25. What this means is that the company will pay up to $50,000 for one injured person, up to $100,000 if there are multiple injuries, and property damage would be limited to $25,000. Split limit liability exposes you to a greater degree of risk than single limit liability, especially in the area of property damage.

Collision insurance also comes into play if you are ever involved in an accident. However, collision insurance only covers the damage that happens to your own car - this is the case if you are at fault or not. This coverage, unfortunately, is not required by law.

Another type of insurance is called comprehension coverage. This covers physical damages to your car that are not the result of a collision, and are not in any way your fault. A tree branch has fallen on your car, someone tossed a brick through the windshield, a part of the car or the car as a whole has been stolen, all of these scenarios fall under comprehension coverage.

Medical payment coverage is in the same ballpark as collision and comprehension coverage. This is because medical coverage insures you and anybody else riding in your car at the time of the accident.

Although many states require every driver to carry liability insurance, the fact remains that a large number of people do not take financial responsibility for their driving privileges. Either they choose to be uninsured or they do something worse like leave the scene of an accident. This failure leaves innocent citizens at great risk of having to pay for medical expenses caused by another person's negligence. When this occurs, some auto insurers make available what is known as uninsured motorist coverage. This is a protection that should always be added to your policy to cover the cost of damages to your car.

Another thing you need to be concerned about is your claims history. An aspect of auto insurance that many consumers do not like is when the company raises premiums due to the number of claims an insured person has filed. Many companies undergo this practice to discourage policy holders from abusing their insurance. Know that as a policy holder, you have the right to file all legitimate claims, and you should not hesitate to do so. Just be aware that some insurance companies are more liberal regarding how they respond to policyholders who file multiple claims within a relatively short period.

Sometimes the insurer will refuse to renew a policy because of a poor driving record. It is possible that no other company will be willing to insure you. There is a solution to this problem. The state insurance departments operate what is called an assigned risk pool. Insurance companies licensed to operate within the state are required to insure drivers on a pooled basis. You will not be able to choose your insurer; instead, one will be assigned to you. The down side of the assigned risk category is the premiums. They are significantly higher than normal rates.

These are the basic and most important types of auto insurance coverages. You can also purchase other relatively minor and inexpensive add-ons called riders or endorsements. An automatic towing service or a car rental service are   two examples of add-ons. These luxuries will be covered by your policy.

But, most importantly, and this cannot be stressed enough, take the time to shop around and   get advice from different agents and companies before you purchase any type of insurance. Not all insurers have the same rates and premiums for identical cars that end up in identical circumstances.

Lastly under the insurance umbrella falls home and property insurance. Property protection reimburses injured parties for losses to their possessions due to fire, loss, or theft. This protection can be extended to include a variety of other disasters. Liability protection covers things that happen to other people, for which you could be held financially responsible.

This insurance comes into play if someone was injured at your residence.

If you carry liability insurance, you would be protected in the event that the injured party needed medical care. You would be covered even if the injured party decided to sue for damages.

Many people are unaware that you do not have to own your own home to benefit from home insurance. Renters insurance covers your personal property and provides liability coverage in the event that someone is injured while visiting you. The industry code for this type of insurance is an HO-4 form.

Standard renter and homeowner policies offer only a minimum of coverage for jewelry and other valuables. If you have valuable items that are sacred to you, identify the items and insure them separately by a policy floater. This name comes from the fact that these items are portable and are insured no matter where you take them. In other words, the policy floats with the items.

Generally those who own their own home have a much larger investment to protect. They also have more to lose financially than those who rent. Not only does the homeowner have valuable personable items, they also own the physical structures - buildings, houses, garages, sheds, workshops, or office spaces. All of these fall under the classification of real property.

Buildings can suffer damage due to a variety of perils. The most comprehensive homeowners policy is an HO-5 form, also called an all-perils policy. It covers all disasters except those specifically excluded by the policy. Typically excluded from the standard homeowners policy are the real threats, such as floods, earthquakes, and other natural disasters. Each of these requires separate and specific coverage.

Other exclusions include the less likely occurrences of war and nuclear accidents. These things fall under a named-perils policy. This type of policy covers a list of clearly identified disasters, and is found on form HO-1.

Form HO-2 is a broad-form policy. When filing a claim, policyholders must prove that their claim resulted from a specifically named peril in their policy. An all-perils policy puts the burden on the insurance company.

Homeowners who borrow money to purchase their homes, then still make mortgage payments are required to insure their property. This is because the lender is the true owner of the property until the debt is paid in full.

Condominium owners purchase homeowners policies coded H0- 6. This policy is specifically designed to insure only what the condominium dweller owns, which is not the building itself. Condominium owners purchase only the space they occupy and personal property.

How much property insurance is needed in this case? The general rule when insuring real property is to insure the property for at least 80% of what it would cost to replace it. The 80% requirement is contained in a co-insurance clause. There is no point in insuring for more than 100% of the replacement cost because insurance companies will not allow you to turn loss into an opportunity for profit.

Suppose that you own real estate valued at $100,000. The buildings on the property would probably cost around $80,000 to replace. The co-insurance clause of your policy requires you to insure your structures for at least $64,000. If you suffer a total loss, the policy will pay the full $80,000.

Something to keep in mind about homeowners insurance is that the insurance company's obligation is only to replace or restore exactly what you lost. Changes to building codes have considerably raised construction costs. There are modest additional premiums that companies will allow you to attach to your policy. This will obligate the company to pay for new construction. This additional coverage is worth the extra premium.

How much personal property insurance? Generally homeowners' policies cover personal contents at %50 of the value of the structure. Therefore, if you insure your home for $80,000, the policy will cover your personal possessions for up to $40,000. The standard homeowners policy covers personal property only at its actual cash value at the time of the loss. You may only be able to get a fraction of its original cost; this is called depreciated value. For a small additional premium, you can purchase replacement cost coverage for your personal property. The insurance company would pay to have your lost items replaced with new ones.

Extended liability coverage will be necessary for securing your life, as well. It is no secret that we live in the age of the lawsuit. Whenever something bad happens to a person, one of their first thoughts is to file suit. A simple way to guard against this is to have an umbrella liability policy. For a relatively low premium, you can purchase a one million dollar liability policy that will sit atop any other policy you may have. It acts as an extension of liability coverage.

If you have $500,000 of liability coverage in your other policies, the umbrella policy will give you a total of $1,500,000 of coverage. Many people in the inner cities treat insurance as a luxury item they can do without. MISTAKE! When budgets get tight, it becomes too easy to ignore those premium notices that come periodically in the mail. Providing adequate insurance to protect yourself, your family, and your property is a necessity of modern life. You should place this expenditure high on your list of financial priorities. You are now becoming a responsible citizen, on your way to fully being able to implement how to S.T.O.P. (Start Thinking Outside Prison)!

S. T. O. P. - START THINKING OUTSIDE PRISON

5

Adjust Your Moral Compass

"Example is not the main thing in influencing others,
it is the only thing . . ."
- Albert Schweitzer

Along with learning the skills of life, comes learning how to conduct yourself towards others. Basically, learning how to align your behavior. What you do and how you act will be projected on others. Setting a good example is important. Thinking outside prison will be an adjustment for you, which will require you to do things that you would have never done in your past life.

Adjusting your moral compass literally means you will separate yourself from all the negative habits the street life attached to you. Then you will have to fill that void with the positive habits that so many rarely practice.

Before making the wrong turn down that dark road to nowhere, you are going to have to make a U-turn. You are going to have to do things differently. For starters - Try not to do things to others that you would not like them to do to you. When doing an injustice, we must take the time to stop and think. How would I like it if this was done to me? Some things in life can't be undone. And not everyone is quick to forgive.

"Do unto others what you would have them do unto you." That has been the golden rule since the beginning of time. Not many can go through life without ever harming anyone. But only a criminal hurts those around him without a second thought. No feelings of guilt, shame, or remorse.

The harm one does to others can recoil on oneself. Not all harmful acts are reversible. You can commit an act against another, which cannot be waived aside or forgotten. Murder is such an act. Killing someone's family member won't be so easily forgiven let alone forgotten.

The ruining of another life can wreck your own. Society reacts against some of the wrong we do. The prisons are full of these examples. Many of us have a family member that has been incarcerated. There are other penalties whether you are caught or not. Committing harmful acts against others, particularly when hidden, can cause you to suffer severe changes in your attitude towards others and yourself.

The happiness and joy of life will soon depart. You will gradually become numb. Try to apply the golden rule to yourself so you can attain a reality of what a harmful act is. Awaken your social consciousness. When you begin to feel no restraint from doing harmful acts, your potential will wither away. Learning how to treat others is important on the road to thinking outside prison.

Holding onto to virtue is also important. Virtues have been attributed to wise men, holy men, and saints. Virtues have made the difference between chaos and a decent society.

Just think about how you would want people to treat you. You would first want to be treated justly. You wouldn't want people lying to you or about you. You wouldn't want to be condemned by anyone. You would want your companions to be loyal. You would not stand for betrayal. You would value

29

good sportsmanship and you would not want to be hoodwinked or tricked.

You would want people to be fair in their dealings with you. You would want them to be honest. When you are feeling down, you would want others to show compassion. Instead of berating you, you probably want others to exhibit self-control. You may want people to be tolerant of your shortcomings and mistakes. You would prefer that people were forgiving, and that they would concentrate less on censure and punishment. You would want others to believe in you and not doubt you at every turn.

You wouldn't wish to be insulted. You would want life and all of its unfolding's to exist on a pleasant level. Indeed you would want all of these things. However, before wanting them, we should try doing them!

Amongst the violence and melodramatic environments we live in, there is a phenomenon at work surrounding human relations. When one person yells at another, the other has an impulse to yell back. A person is pretty much treated the way he treats others. In actuality, one can set the example of how he wishes to be treated.

Joy and pleasure do not come from immorality. It is quite the reverse. Joy and pleasure are deeply rooted within honest hearts. An immoral heart, on the other hand, will experience joy at times, but it will always end up with the thing it finds most attractive. Things like tragedy, suffering, and pain. True virtue has very little to do with gloominess. True virtue is the bright face of life itself.

What do you suppose would happen if you treated those around you with justice, loyalty, good sportsmanship, fairness, honesty, kindness, consideration, compassion, self-control, tolerance, forgiveness, benevolence, belief, respect, politeness, dignity, admiration, friendliness, love, and did all of this with integrity? It may take a while, but others would eventually began treating you the same way.

You can certainly influence the conduct of others around you, if you are not doing that already. You can start by picking one virtue a day. Practice it. Incorporate it into your actions. It is certain that your character and personality will change.

Aside from personal benefit, you can take hold of someone's hand, no matter how small, and begin a new era for human relations. A pebble dropped in the ocean can send ripples to the farthest shore. Set the tone; how you treat people and how you demand to be treated is pertinent to your success.

Acting kindly towards people isn't enough. There must be sincerity behind each action. In order to be trusted, one must first prove him or herself trustworthy. People are going to disappoint us. But that disappointment can be easily overcome as long as we can trust the people around us. Mutual trust is the firmest building block in human relations. Without it, the whole structure comes down.

When you are considered a trustworthy person, you have value. Without it, you are not worth much to anyone, except to other untrustworthy people. So set standards for the people around you. Make them earn your respect and your trust. It's not going to happen overnight; so don't get discouraged. A trusting relationship develops with one small gesture at a time.

One way to gain trust is to hold true to your word. No matter how great or small, if you say you are going to do a thing... try your utmost to do it. And, if for some reason you fail, if for some reason beyond your control you are not able to keep your word, an earnest person will recognize your earnest efforts. This of course is only true if you keep earnest people around you. You will need reliable and honest people when you begin readjusting to society.

A sure way to influence the people around you is to set a good example. In this age of technology, someone is ALWAYS watching you. The old, the young... people will be paying attention to your behavior. Some will want to see you fail. Others would love for you to prosper. Law officials already expect you to return home as the same loser you were before you went to prison. You owe it to yourself – and to the brothers and sisters still incarcerated - to be a good representative of positive change. This will help convince the law officials and society that we can come home and be productive.

There may be some little kid who does not want to be the latest athlete, rapper or movie star. They may want to be just like you when they grow up. Influence affects countless people, and you never know who those people are going to be. If you set the good example, others around you will immediately feel your influence.

Of course there will be those who will not like or appreciate this change within you. They would much rather you return to your old self. If this is the case, then these people factually mean you harm, and you need to be rid of them. Deep down, these people have some level of respect for you, but they are too afraid to admit it. Hold true to your values, your virtues, and your standards. Continue setting the good example and no one will be able to stop you from achieving S.T.O.P.! The main ones that need your influence are the children. They soak up everything like sponges. Their development needs positive influence, simply because today's children will be tomorrow's adults. What society puts into them is exactly what society will get out of them.

The inner city and the projects can be hostile, miserable, and negative places to be reared. Many of the children who grow up in these places are held without love, proper care, and guidance. The majority of them grow up angry, bitter, and confused. Believe me! I know from experience.

I was about 19 or 20. I was trafficking drugs in this small town of York, Pennsylvania. I ended up meeting a young woman; I can't even begin to describe her beauty, but I'll try. She had a butter pecan complexion and a shapely body. Her hair was jet black and it spilled all the way to the middle of her back. I was young and vibrant, and the only thing I had concern for was getting in her Victoria Secrets!

That was accomplished fairly easily. She was attracted to me and the life I was living. She had taken me to her house where she resided with her cousin. Her cousin had a two-year-old daughter, and I never paid much attention to the little girl during my first few visits. While I came in and out of town doing my dirt, this woman's house became my rest haven. The relationship quickly developed. This butter pecan girl began wanting more and more.

She was 32 with a lot of qualities I admired, but my lifestyle simply wouldn't allow it. I enjoyed the sex, but that's all it was. However, during one of my daytime visits, I was sitting in the front room, while my lady friend was making breakfast. I began to observe the little girl. She was in the same corner I had seen her on many of my previous visits. It struck me odd because she didn't speak much for a two-year-old. No words, she didn't grunt, she didn't even breathe loud! I had a weakness for women and children. Naturally, I began trying to communicate with the little girl. I spoke to her softly with gentle words, but the girl remained distant and silent.

As time went on, I realized that no one in the house showed any real concern for the girl. When they did, it was only to yell at her. The little girl had built a wall around herself to keep everyone out. Even the people who were trying to be nice to her. Not a lot of yelling was going on when I was present in the house. I used to check the adults with quickness! I would say, "try talking calmly to the girl. She can still understand you without all that screaming."

At that moment, I realized how important the male role is in the household. The little girl noticed it, too. When I would stop the women from shouting at her, she would look across the room with a look of appreciation and security on her face. She still hadn't warmed up to me yet. As far as I could tell, she had watched all the male figures she had ever known walk right out the door - none of them showing any concern for her.

I made it my business to bring a smile to this little girl's face. I started bringing her new toys and candy. She wouldn't accept anything from me at first, so I used to just set the gifts next to her on the floor and leave. When I would come back later, she would be eating the candy or playing with the toy. I would happily greet the little girl whenever I came in, and I would make sure I gave her a pleasant farewell whenever I left. Still, she resisted my friendship.

One day, I came in the house and I did my usual by giving her a present. Only a few seconds after sitting down, the little girl walked right up to my knee. She just stood there. I guess that was her sign of approval. I asked if I could hold her, and she raised her arms. She still wouldn't talk a lot, but I realized that the little girl had always understood me since the moment I had shown her kindness.

My lady friend didn't have any children, so we used to take this little girl to the park and store with us. One day, I was preparing to leave the house, and the girl ran up to me crying because she wanted to go with me. It gave me a sad feeling because I knew my lifestyle would not allow me to play daddy. Speaking of which, I always wondered, "where was this little girl's father?"

Today's children are tomorrow's civilization. But bringing a child into this world nowadays is like dropping them into the lion's den. Children can't handle their environment and they have no real resources. A child is like a blank slate, if you write the wrong thing on it the child will begin to say and do the wrong things. But, unlike a slate, a child can begin to do its own writing. The problem is that the child starts to write what has already been written.

Most children are capable of great decency. At the same time, many are born with mental problems or even born as drug addicts. Some are simply neglected, like the little girl I met those many years ago.

Children need positive role models and good friends in their lives. We can be the role models and we can be the friends. We should try to find out what a child's problem really is. Kids have solutions to their own issues, but often times we crush them because we don't understand them. We should observe them better, even the babies. Listen to what children tell us about their lives. Let them help us! If you don't, they become over-whelmed with obligations they must repress. A child, factually, does not do well without love. Most children have an abundance of love to return. Teach them, love them, guide them, and show them how important they really are. S.T.O.P. is about giving back to the community. Are the children not part of that community?

Children are essential for a better future, so too are the parents. We should revert back to honoring and helping them. This requires listening to them. As young people we don't understand certain things, so we rebel against the wisdom of our parents. We don't fully understand that most parents have their children's best interest at heart. When we run away from home or drop out of school, or hang out with people our parents told us were no good: that's when we realize we made a wrong turn. The path we have gone down is slippery. Before we know it, we are somewhere our soul really doesn't want to be such as prison, the crack house, on welfare, impoverished, and near death both mentally and physically.

We should go back and recapture the wisdom our parents were trying to give us when we were children. They still have much to offer. But they won't be around forever. I lost my father while incarcerated. I feel like there is so much more I need to ask him. I remember one of our final visits at the prison. He shook my hand instead of giving me a hug. I think that's when he began to acknowledge the man in me.

Parents are difficult to understand from a child's point of view. There are differences between generations. Parents are almost always acting from a very strong desire to do what they believe to be best for their child. We are indebted to our parents from start to finish. Some parents aren't in it for the return. Nevertheless, there will come a time when the younger generation will have to care for the older generation. They are the only parents we have. We should, no matter what, honor and help them.

It's all a part of moral conduct - treating others the right way, guiding children toward the right way, and giving proper respect to our parents and those in authority.

6

Practice Your Principles

"Believe nothing, no matter where you read
it, or who said it, no matter if I have said it,
unless it agrees with your own reason and
your own common sense . . ."
-The Buddha

Thinking outside of prison will come with principles. You will begin to see things in a different light. Breaking the law must not be so impulsive for you anymore. You must learn to become more temperate and competent. You can no longer get drunk all night and stand on the corner with the fellas. Your responsibilities will require you to act more competently.

One of the first things you will need to practice is being temperate. Knowing how to do things in moderation is important. It wouldn't be wise to take a mind altering substance. 9 out of 10 people end up incarcerated, while they are under the influence of something. People who take drugs do not always see the real world in front of them. You are not yourself at the moment you get high. Even when you are not high, you are probably looking for ways to get high. You mistakenly believe you feel better or act better, or perhaps you think you are only happy when on drugs. This is just another delusion. Sooner or later, the drugs will destroy you physically.

When a person begins to practice their principles, the miracles that occur in their life is amazing. I take my aunt for example. All my life, I have known her to get high off heavy drugs. However, when I turned 17, she made a complete 360° turn around. She has been clean now for over 15 years. She also cut out all the side dishes, drinking alcohol and smoking ciga-rettes.

She is in her 50's now and well-accomplished. I've never seen her happier. During her sober years, she went back to school and got her GED, then went on to get an associate's degree. In addition to that, she just finished 4 years of college with credentials aimed at the medical field. This is a prime example of how one should just S.T.O.P.!

Throughout my aunt's struggles, she never spent any time in prison. She may have come close on a few occasions, but she was able to recognize her problems and get on the right track before she ever had a chance to reach prison. With more people like my aunt and programs like S.T.O.P., we can crush the recidivism here in America.

Don't think that just because you drink, but don't do drugs that you are okay and don't have a problem. People who consume alcohol are not alert. It impairs your ability to react, even when it seems to you that you are more alert because of it. My father, R.I.P., used to tell me when he got himself clean, "In order to get over, you'll need to be sober," and "Life will pass you by if you are always high." I stand on those principles to this day in honor of my father's name.

Not doing anything illegal is a principle you will need to put into effect im-mediately. The risk is always greater than the reward when you are doing crime. When I wasn't thinking outside of prison, I had found myself doing foul things that eventually appeared normal to me. I had become submis-sive to my environment and numb to my behavior.

A person will forget that laws exist, that is until those handcuffs get slapped on those wrists. Ignorance is no excuse for breaking the law. Every member of society has a responsibility, whether young or old, to know what society considers to be an illegal act. When you commit a crime, small or big, you are laid open to an attack by the state. The state and government tend to work as a rather unthinking machine. This machine exists to work on laws and codes of laws. It is geared toward striking down all channels of illegality. As such, it can be an implacable enemy. Strangely enough, the rightness and incorrectness of a thing does not seem to count in the face of the law.

When you realize that those around you are committing crimes, you should do what you can to discourage them and at the same time get completely away from the situation. You may not be a party to it, but you can suffer because of it. There are plenty of people in prison solely based on conspiracy, even if they knew what was going on or not. So, make it a part of your principles to see that children and adults alike are informed of what is legal and illegal.

Also, make sure everyone around you clearly understands that you do not engage in illegal acts. "All men are equal under the law" is a principle, which in its own time and place of tyranny and aristocracy, was one of the greatest social advances in human history. No one should lose sight of this. Now, the opportunities we have in life are endless, despite the insistence of evil men that all men are evil.

There are many good men and women around. You have been fortunate enough to have known some. The company you keep will play a major part in your ability to S.T.O.P. The principles you now subscribe to should not allow you to hang out with drug dealers or anyone else who commits crimes. Your principles should take you to places where you are held accountable like work, school, family, and home. Being competent in these areas should give you the knowledge to look, learn, and practice.

Man began to dominate his environment once he learned to think, value knowledge, and apply that knowledge toward skill. Being competent means to make your own observations. All too often we take society's views or the views of our peers, which can influence your thinking and your actions. See what you see, not what someone tells you to see. What you observe is what you observe. View things, life, and others directly. Not through any cloudy, prejudice curtain of fear or another's interpretation. A child or an adult sees what he or she sees and that is their reality. True competence is based on one's own ability to observe.

The main process of learning consists of inspecting, selecting truth from falsehood, the important from the unimportant, ultimately arriving at conclusions you can apply. If you do this, you are well on your way to being competent enough to start thinking outside prison.

The process of learning is not just piling data on top of more data. Rather, it is obtaining new understanding and better ways to do things. Those who do well in life never really stop studying and learning. It is a very arrogant person who thinks he or she has nothing further to learn in life. The most hardened criminals never learned how to learn or think. Repeatedly, the courts seek to teach that if you commit the crime again, you will go back to prison. Most of us are victims of this repetitive foolishness. Our lack of self-control, realistic principles, and the inability to think is the deciding factor for how the majority of laws are passed through Congress. They base their findings off the stupidity of criminals!

Factually, criminals are causing the passing of more and more laws. The decent citizen is the one that obeys the law, while the criminals, by definition, do not. Lawbreakers possess an inability to learn. Orders, directives, punishments or any other form of duress will not work upon a being that does not know how to learn. Especially those that lack true principles. The insane cannot learn. They are driven by hidden, evil intentions and are crushed beyond the ability to reason. They personify false data. They will not, or cannot, perceive or learn.

A multitude of personal and social problems arise from the inability or refusal to learn. The lives of those around you have gone off the track, because they do not know how to better themselves through study and learning. Your newfound principles should help you to help those around you acquire knowledge that will improve them.

As we know, life is largely trial and error. Instead of coming down on an incompetent person who has made a mistake, find the reason the mistake was made in the first place. How else can we determine if the person can learn from it? This gives us a chance to bring another person to a competent level of thinking. You may be able to untangle another person's life just by getting them to study, learn, practice, and think.

There are many ways to do this, but being gentle and kind works best. The world is brutal and cruel enough toward people who can't learn and think. Teaching others should be a part of your principles. Learning bears fruit when it is applied.

Wisdom, of course, can be pursued for its own sake. There is even beauty in it. But, truth be told, one can never know if he is wise or not until his learning is applied, then the results of that application can be seen. With age comes wisdom. A thirty-year-old should not be thinking the same way he or she did when they were twenty. A person's know-how must be brought up to speed with their current age. This is done with practice.

One can train their body - eyes, hands, feet, etc., until they can develop a natural reaction in some situations. Like a boxer, for example, repetitive training will allow you to block and throw a punch when necessary. In any activity, much of what passes for talent is really practice. You must work on each movement by doing it over and over, until you can get it done accurately without even thinking about it.

The same concept applies to crafts and professions. The lawyer who has not practiced courtroom procedures may not have learned to shift his or her mental gears fast enough to defend an attack and win a case. A salesman or stockbroker who has not rehearsed selling can lose a fortune in minutes. This is why practice is important.

You must practice executing your plan every day. Get up each morning with the same goals in mind. It is the consistency of the process that will enhance the practice. For an ex-con, this world will be totally new for you. It will take some practice and getting used to the high-speed world of getting up and going to work every day.

The main objective is to practice and stick to your principles. People around you, mainly your old friends, will try to hand you back your old contract, which was your old way of living. You must show your friends and family that you live a new life and that your views are now different, because they will be waiting for signs of the old you to resurface. Weakness is easily penetrated. Hold firm to your standards and do not bend under any circumstance. Stick to practicing the principles you now stand upon. And make sure those in your circle are doing the same. Keep in mind that your principles can become corrupted by the people in your life. A police officer who honors his badge is not going to hang around a stick-up kid, just as a lion is not going to hang with a house-trained dog.

Finding something to do with your leisure time will be important. People get in the most trouble when they don't know what to do with idle time. There is a lot of "clean" fun one can indulge in - a family night of playing cards, the bowling alley, skating rink, and many other things.

In order to practice your principles precisely, you must stay out of your old neighborhood and other areas that helped develop your past habits. A recovering alcoholic has no business sitting in a liquor store. A recovering gambler has no business going to Vegas. I never understood why I was stuck in a rut of going to jail, wasting my money, and wasting my time. I had to end up in prison to finally realize that I needed to change the places I had frequented and the people around me. But, every time I came home from jail, I rushed right back to my psychological drug, which were the projects in Orange, New Jersey, 325 and 108. I treated it like it was the last place on earth.

Even when I was doing dirt out of state or simply just visiting family, I couldn't wait to get back to the projects. That place was my magnet! Other than prison, I have never seen a place so lacking in morals and principles. Many of my former associates are unfortunately stuck in that same rut. Most of them are in prison or dead. A good thing about prison is that it will allow you time to truly find yourself.

I chose a different path than my former associates. A person on the ground should only be concerned with getting up. I felt the only thing that could save me would be a significant change. I had taken my family and myself through enough agony and heartache. Finding myself really gave me an understanding of having principles.

I had a false belief about what principles really were. It is a person with no morals that leaves their families to run the streets with their so-called friends. It is a person with no principles that will rob and kill a child or old person. The same sort of person spends so much time in jail that they are not around to raise their children properly. They will spend all their money getting drunk and high, knowing their baby needs diapers or the bills need to be paid. Understanding what principles are will help us begin to practice and stick to them. Your principles are part of the foundation you will need to S.T.O.P.!

7

Assert Your Values

"A friend is someone who knows you as
you are, understands where you've been,
accepts who you've become, and still
invites you to grow."
- Stu Weber, "Locking Arms"

Get with the program. Life doesn't revolve around one individual. It is a collective whole that makes the world turn. As you re-enter society, your approach must be to support your government and to repair and safeguard your community by fulfilling your obligations.

Look at government and politics from a prisoner's point of view. You will probably hate everyone from the White House to the warden at the prison. This is because everything a prisoner stands for is opposed by society. What we fail to understand is that passing laws through Congress and the treatment of prisoners is all designed to structure your value system.

Some don't ever understand this fact. We tend to play the victim, but victimize everything in sight. Once you change, you must begin to assert your value system. Not only by speaking against what you used to be, but by becoming the solution to the many problems the world faces.

Nowadays, too many people have very little value on life, somebody else's life or their own life, for that matter. They have never been taught how to value something as precious as a life. Anyone who comes to understand the concept of S.T.O.P. will be responsible for asserting his or her value system, along with the other lessons you may learn on your journey toward change.

I challenge you to be responsible for the youth. I also challenge you to change the negative thinking in every criminal you come in contact with. Let them know that there is a better way to live and be happy. It starts with becoming part of the system that many dislike so much. Let the world know that you stand for something, that you are proud to be an American, that you value your country and fellow Americans.

Be a part of the positive peer pressure group. There is already so much negativity in our communities that the children aren't allowed the room they need to blossom. Before we know it, Little Garry becomes Lil' G. His pants are sagging. His speech is inappropriate and unintelligible. Thus, he is selling drugs at thirteen or in a gang!

It's up to us to assert our values and let them know that it is okay to be different. There should be no reason to lose our children to the system or no reason they lose their lives because of stray bullets. Little Garry or 72-year-old Ms. Edna should not be afraid to sit on the porch due to gun violence.

Thinking outside of prison can be hard to accomplish when shadowed by the oppression of tyranny. A benign government designed to protect all people deserves the necessary support of its citizens to smooth the way. Our president (at the time of this writing), Barack Obama, is working hard for the change of all people. It doesn't seem to me that he is working for the special interest of just one group. Rather he is catering to the fairness of everyone. He should receive all of our support to the fullest.

The concept of government (civics) comprises a great many things - political economy, political philosophy, political power, etc. It is almost a technical science, theorized through the ideas of men. It is the individual, you, me, all of us whose opinion matters most. Let's assert our principles from the bottom all the way to the top of the chain.

Of all the values we assert within ourselves, our appearance is one of the most important. Often, we get judged off of first impression. The concept of looking presentable has long since left our communities. My parents, yours too, used to seem like they were always dressed up. Daddy always wore the suit and tie. Mommy was always in a dress. Sagging pants and women wearing clothing that appears like another layer of skin have replaced those qualities.

It's a nice visual, but when I look deeper, I see low self-esteem, confusion, low values, low morals, and no self-respect. We should encourage the people around us to look more presentable. Compliment a person when he or she looks nice. Even better, help them with their problem when they can't help themselves. That small act may improve their self-regard and their morals.

Taking care of your community should be a part of your value system as well. I remember growing up in the projects with writing all over the walls. Every so often, the building would get painted from top to bottom. Within a month, the vandalism would resurface. There was urine in the hallways and garbage in the stairwell. The way the place looked was the way everyone acted! We must protect our possessions, and then get everyone else to protect theirs.

Another thing that needs protecting is the planet. No earth means no you or me. To share this planet means that we should help care for it. What happens on the other side of the world can effect what happens in your own home. Scientific findings through space probes have determined that our world can deteriorate and no longer support life. It could happen during your lifetime. Cut down too many forests or foul too many rivers and seas and there you have it. The surface temperature becomes roasting hot. The rain turns to sulfuric acid. Eventually, all living things will die. Man has reached the potential to destroy this planet, but we must push ourselves toward the actions of saving it.

We can do many things that will help take care of this planet. One thing we can do is own the idea that you HAVE TO take care of it. Then suggest to others that they do the same. Our obligations since birth are to the earth and the creatures on it.

Maintaining an industrious attitude is also key. Work is not always pleasant, but few are unhappier than those who lead a purposeless, idle existence. The retired person with nothing further to accomplish perishes due to inactivity. But simply getting busy at something can ease sorrow itself. Morale is boosted to its highest heights by accomplishments. In fact, it can be demonstrated that production is the basis of morale.

Be mindful that every new value you obtain may not coincide with the values of everyone else. Whatever you stand for, however, be sure to assert it endlessly. Others will still try to crush your hopes and dreams. They will be set on watching you fail. They will use you as the object of their attack just so they can try to improve their own lives. When faced with these types of situations, asserting your values must never be abandoned.

S.T.O.P. is also about flourishing and prospering. It's about learning the proper life skills and adjusting your character to function as a normal U.S. citizen. It's about practicing the tools you have acquired to become spiritually, mentally, physically, and financially successful. We cannot allow anyone to stampede upon what we believe. These are our values we are talking about here.

Some will share our ideas, some won't. The ones who won't will be those who have yet to start thinking outside prison. These very people will consider you a square. They will use every tempting avenue to lure you back into your old life.

There is only one way to handle these types of people - that is to remain flourishing and prospering. We all know the saying, "Success is the best revenge." Don't give up just because you have haters; that's what they want you to do. Just keep on "doing you" as the young people say. The haters will eventually go into a state of apathy. They will give up hating completely once they see they can't break you. Remember, your goals in life are worthwhile. Success means you will wind up the victor in the long run. Only you are able to choose the road you wish to travel in life.

Life is not a calm and orderly thing. There will be highs and lows. Some may even think that they have been on the low road for so long that it is too late for them to make a change. There is no person alive who is incapable of making a new beginning. One can always reinvent his or herself as long as they stand for something. Losses and setbacks will happen; just learn from them. All roads have bumps. But it can still be traveled. You'll fall down, but that's the only way to get back on your feet. Your values must be strong enough to carry you through.

During my incarceration, most people thought I was crazy. I don't know, maybe it was because I used to move with a purpose in a purposeless environment. An ambitious person with values will most certainly stand out amongst his or her peers. People will say that you are crazy too. Some will believe that you think you are better than everyone else. I didn't allow such things to sidetrack me. My goal was greater. I even created a favorite slogan during those challenging times. I would literally tell people, "My agenda is greater than you."

All I could see was that three-decade sentence the judge handed me. And I was determined to make that sentence disappear or decrease. For that to happen, I knew that my value system had to change. I was in the "House of Pain" known as New Jersey State Prison where misery comes in all forms. I began to assert my value system. I stuck to the script, no matter what, day in and day out.

I stopped playing basketball. I stopped going to the yard all the time and turned my cell into my own planet fitness. I was much better off with less interaction. Some prison activities are grounds for individuals to release their misery. The big yard and the gymnasium were two of those places. My intention was to get rid of the time I had to do, not to gain more. I stood clear of religious services after a while. I realized that if I became a part of a group, then I would be taking on whatever problems that group had to face. I made the decision to stand on my own; that way all the problems that came my way were because of me and me only. I even avoided the mess hall, another breeding ground for misery. The food wasn't enough to sustain a child, let alone a grown man.

I had so-called friends try to pull me off my square. They tried to derail me from my daily habits and encourage me to do what they thought I should be doing. Some didn't understand. Some did, and those were the ones that I clung to.

I did my best to rid myself of any filthy habits. I began keeping the company of men who would frequent the law library or educational programs. My entire approach to doing time changed, and the judicial system certainly took notice. They began engaging me with psychological games. I knew, but I didn't care. My mission was still the same - get my black ass out of prison!

Asserting your values means knowing what needs to be done, then doing it in a vigorous manner. Let the people around you know what you are about. Do this through your actions and not just words. The same way of thinking applies outside prison as well. If one wants to excel, then one has to prioritize and place his values in the forefront. Coming to prison really taught me what was important about being free. When I was running the streets, I didn't value women. But, in prison, a man will write every girl he knows a ten-page letter professing just how much he deeply loves them.

Before incarceration, prisoners would run in and out of mommy's house. And there would be times when mommy wouldn't see us for weeks. But, once we come to prison, we become the perfect son. And still, every letter and phone call is asking mommy and daddy to send us this, send us that. Prison just has a blunt way of showing a person what truly should be valued. Prison will teach you that your friends on the street weren't really your friends. Some may have been true friends. But ask yourself... where are they now?

The best way to win is to assert your values. Mean what you say and say what you mean. Be the man you are supposed to be. Value your system of doing things. If you have a wife and children, make sure you spend time with them at home instead of running the streets. If you have a job, arrive at work early or at least be on time. Whatever your obligations are, fulfill them as best as you can. Once you veer off the road of fulfilling your responsibilities, your value system will depreciate.

Your positive habits can actually become like a plague that can influence other men to be assertive. A movement starts with a single thought from one individual. This sparks inspiration in others and encouragement to become a part of a beautiful thing.

There comes a point in life when one must say "enough is enough!" Drugs, violence, recidivism... these things must be drowned and buried. The best way to achieve this is to assert your values. The values of positive thinking and productivity can alleviate many of the problems in today's society. To do that, there must be more people willing to assert what is right. History proves that change is inevitable. So, S.T.O.P., promote and become a part of the change by letting your values shine through.

8

Keep Your Eyes On The Prize

"Failure is the greatest opportunity to
know who I really am."
- John Killinger

What is the use of setting goals if you never accomplish them? What sense does it make to reach the pinnacle of life only to throw it away on one bad decision? We are all distracted by one thing or another. Some distractions are merely for the moment and others last a lifetime. When a distraction impedes our ambition to succeed, then we are definitely focused on the wrong things.

When we were children, our vision was quite clear. The passing years, however, has made it difficult to see what is at the end of the tunnel. The ability to see straight has been drastically impaired. Everything on the road-side is more attractive than traveling the road itself. The prize at the end is no longer a concern.

Any athlete understands the significance of forward motion. Boxing, foot-ball, basketball, soccer, hockey... all sports require moving straight ahead to achieve success. The same rule applies to non-athletes. We must keep our eyes forward to keep ourselves moving forward.

The roadside causes us to lose control and self-destruct before we even set eyes on the prize. And this isn't the prize one may find in the bottom of a cereal box. This prize is one's success and happiness, then being able to share that success with someone else. Some are going to fall a few times along the journey, but those who keep looking ahead are the ones who will get back up. The rest will be distracted. Boyfriends and girlfriends are now more important than goals. Substance abuse becomes a crutch. Then the carriage gets put before the horse. This is when the hardships begin, and one can't see beyond their own nose.

Sadly, the carriage can't pull the horse because life has a natural order for everything, including reaching success. Ideally the order is to wreak all kinds of havoc as a child. Grow out of it. Finish high school. Go to college or learn a trade. Even start a business. By one's late twenties or early thir-ties, marriage should be on the horizon. Then come the children, the house, and some other finer things life may have to offer. The prize is so close at this point that one shouldn't need glasses to see it.

You don't want to do things in any other order. Don't have three kids before learning advanced algebra. Don't have children at an age where you can still be called a child yourself. Welfare, minimum wage, barely getting by... these are all terms that come to mind when the natural order is disturbed. Anyone would have trouble focusing under these circumstances.

Your eyes may be on the prize, but the people around you may be focusing on something else entirely. Either you're going to affect them positively or they're going to have a negative effect on you; the latter is more likely to happen.

True story... I met a young lady when I was sixteen. I was on the brink of dropping out of school and didn't know the direction my life was headed. I had become a full time drug dealer, who was addicted to marijuana, and a ruthless street thug. This young lady, on the other hand, was three years older than me. She was beautiful and vibrant. She had already finished high school and was deep into her second year of college. She was childless, working a full time job, and paying for her own apartment. On all levels, she was an idiot's dream girl, but a real man's prize.

Unfortunately, I was an idiot at the time. I just happened to be handsome, seemingly mature for my age with money and charm. The young lady felt herself becoming attached to me. She would pull back, knowing deep within herself that I was the wrong guy to be involved with. Attraction is powerful, however. She lived her normal life, and I continued creating havoc in the streets, yet we stayed together. I even tried to tell her that I was no good for her, but she didn't listen. Hell, I did what any fool would have done; I pulled her down the road I was traveling. Of course I was unaware of it at the time, but that's no excuse. She began doing things to impress me with her money. I didn't know it, but she was getting behind in all her bills because she was trying to live how I lived. She began tagging along whenever I hit the block. She neglected school. She even wasted most of her tuition money by bailing me out of jail on occasion.

She became clingy. A burden. I cheated on her right to her face just to push her away, but it didn't work. I believe she became mesmerized by the thrill of street life. Sitting in hospitals while I recovered from being shot or stabbed, watching me fight other dudes in the street - these nonsensical things became a rush to her.

Eventually she dropped out of college, lost her apartment, moved back with her grandmother, and was barely getting by on a minimum wage job. Chasing my whereabouts became her part time occupation, along with drinking, bar hopping, club hopping, and hanging out with people who were just like her. I must say, she proved to be a "ride or die" chick. Five years into my prison stint, our relationship ended. Her bright future was also ended, all my fault of course, but she was the one who had taken her eyes off her own prize.

There is no resurrection. There is only one opportunity to enjoy this life. To receive the fullness of what life has to offer, one must keep their eyes on the prize. What you want out of life should be first priority. People are going to be disappointed, but your loyalty must remain with your true friends and family. These are the people who will encourage you to reach a level of greatness and help you along the way.

If you start thinking outside of prison, the system won't receive decades of your life before you finally wake up. You won't end up in a relationship with someone that was going nowhere in the first place.

The plan should be simple. From birth to around age 12, a child is completely dependent upon its parents. This is the time to just simply be a kid.

From 13 to 17, the influence of responsible adults is key. This is when a child is being groomed to know what the prize is so they can keep their eyes on it. Between 17 and 30 is where things get a bit tricky. During this period, the child, who is now a young adult, will be making more of its own decisions. The future literally gets decided during this period, which covers a lot of ground. A career is possibly chosen. Kids, planned or unplanned, seem to pop up. Large purchases dictate the spending - house, apartment, car, etc. Then there is the possible mate that may come into a person's life. Crucial and careful decision making during this time will be the only thing that will allow a person to keep their eyes on the prize.

30 and 40 is where the battle testing comes into play. However, focus should not and cannot be changed. A person just has to accept the fact that relationships fail. Debts and bills take over. Responsibility becomes overbearing.

If we haven't found the prize by our 40's of 50's, it should definitely be right around the corner. But, even with the prize at the tip of your fingertips, these times could still be a test. This is the age when the parent now becomes dependent upon the child. Senior family members may die. At this age, a person's children may be having children of their own. The proverbial mid-life crisis may be coming to town. A person could look in the mirror and not recognize his or her self. They certainly won't see the person they were twenty years ago.

If this time period is survived, the next ten or so years should be easy sailing. Retirement should be on the horizon. No more working endless hours to make ends meet because the money should be making money by now. The horse will be pulling the cart with little to no effort now. You put in all the work and kept your focus where it should have been. You pushed yourself through the trying times, even when you couldn't see the hidden dangers. We wanted to throw in the towel, but we didn't. We realized that life is like a bank, you have to put something in it to get something out of it.

And what we get out of it is success. A person needs to define their own success. For example, I had a childhood friend named Derrick Byrd. Derrick played four years of Division One basketball for Auburn University. His team even made it to the Final 4 in 2003. He and I had once played on the same 7th-grade basketball team. He ran the point, and I was the shooting guard. Neither one of us made it to the NBA. My choices led me to prison. Derrick's choices allowed him to rely on his Auburn degree. He earns upward of six figures. Now, some would say that the NBA would have been the ultimate success for Derrick, but Derrick defined success for himself. He listened when his parents taught him to keep his eyes on the prize.

I knew another young brother named Cory Boyd. we grew up in the same housing projects. I had the privilege of watching him go from Pee Wee Pop

Warner football to being an explosive running back for South Carolina. Then I watched him get drafted by the Denver Broncos. What's important about all of this is that he kept his eyes on the prize since the age of six! I was a little older than Cory at the time and I used to watch him walk from practice every day. I even threw him a few passes whenever I would see him carrying his football. Of course I was already selling drugs at the time. Our focus was so different that he rushed for a thousand yards on the field while I watched him do it from my prison cell.

We should pay attention to the success of others. We have stories on end about people's failures, too many to count. It is individuals like Derrick and Cory that can actually teach us something. Shadow the life of a successful person. Take their advice and avoid their mistakes. If you see that someone failed because of drug use, why make the same mistake? If you see numerous people drink their life away, why make the same mistake? If your cousin sold drugs and ended up with ten years in prison, why follow him? If your brother or sister was in a relationship that was abusive on all levels, why not avoid those types of relationships? If you know that dropping out of high school was the beginning of your parents' demise, then why make the same mistake. If promiscuity and unprotected sex increases the odds for contracting HIV, then why be a senseless whore monger?

I know why. We're invincible. What happened to them won't happen to us. We got it like that. THAT'S NOT TRUE AT ALL! NOT EVEN A LITTLE BIT! At some point in life, the people who didn't ask themselves these questions took their eyes off the prize. They didn't focus and work hard when they were young so they could reap the benefit when they were older. They didn't sell themselves short by buying a car they couldn't afford. They didn't opt for the designer clothes when they knew lesser brands looked just as good. They understood that it wasn't the car or the clothes that was important, it was the person driving the car and wearing the clothes. Their prize was worth keeping an eye on.

GOAL
VISION
MISSION
STRATEGY
IMPLEMENTATION
SUCCESS

9

Teach The Youth

"I believe that children are our future. Teach
them well and let them lead the way . . ."
- Whitney Houston

Adults need to shape the way for children. What if a child never had to experience a loved one going to prison? The child's mind would have an undamaging understanding of prison. Children mimic adults. What we portray is inflicted upon the child.

Right now, the future of the youth is in trouble. Boys are becoming too feminine and girls are becoming to masculine. This is largely due to the adults of the genders not performing their roles. Boys are being raised by women and girls are being raised by men. The children don't receive the balance of a two-parent home, thus confusion is the result.

If a cat is born, yet raised around dogs, the cat will try to bark even though it doesn't have the capability. The same concept can be applied to children. They tend to mimic their surroundings. If a young boy watches his mother pamper her nails, he becomes interested in the same kind of things. The boy may become too concerned with his outer appearance. Then he watches his mother handle situations with her emotions. He may see his mother argue or gossip. He may witness her using her feminine wiles to survive in the world. The boy, due to no fault of his own, will take on the same survival skills. This is all he knows. This is all he was taught.

Confusion sets in once the boy is no longer around his mother. He will be forced into the reality that he is a boy and that he is absolutely different from his mother. The world will treat him like a man, but he will respond with the characteristics of a woman. His mother can teach him a lot, but there is no way for her to teach him how to become a man.

Today so many young boys are interested in watching soap operas. Some are overly concerned with their nails and hair or other aspects of their outer appearance. Some engage in loud and wild verbal disputes, all of which are things he very well may have learned from his mother. He had no father to teach him the difference between a flathead   or a Phillips screwdriver. No one taught him how to ride or fix his bike. The boy had nothing to imitate but his mother. There are women in the world who can teach a boy these things; but, if they were a single parent, they didn't have time to teach the boy much. The boy only learned what he saw. The men who would have normally influenced him are either in prison, dead, or gay.

The young girls are not faring much better. They find themselves in and out of relationships, trying to discover what they should look for in a man. They watched their mother traipse from one man to the next. They watched her fail and maybe become bitter towards all men. The young girls think this is normal behavior or that their mother actually likes this sort of thing. Eventually, they adopt the same way of thinking. They think that their mother gets a man and then gets rid of him because she doesn't need him. Who do the young girls turn to for answers? Other young girls, that's who.

On the other side of things, if both parents were in the home, then the young boy and girl have a chance to fare much better. The boy will develop his masculinity - learn to fix things around the house and how to be a protector and provider for his family. He will learn how to treat a woman. The young girl will discover her natural inclination towards being a nurturer. She will learn what to expect of a man and how to complement him. Both will learn that one completes the other.

Sadly our children are not getting a fair start. The foundation from day one is not grounded. With nothing to keep the children on the ground, the boy will hit the streets running at full speed where all the attractions of death and danger will be awaiting him. The things the father was supposed to teach him will be discovered the hard way, or be discovered too late.

The girl will do the same thing, and the dangers that await her are far more grave than what awaits the boy. A woman can do a great deal on her own. But, whether she wants to admit it or not, she must have a man to attain true completeness. Just as there is no completeness for the man without her.

This is one of the missing lessons for our children today. They are falsely being taught that they can survive without the knowledge of how a girl becomes a woman or a boy becomes a man. The entire community must shoulder the task of mentoring and guiding the youth. The youth must be taught to realize their importance.

The young must learn that prison is not a thing to be glorified. It's not a badge of honor nor is it any kind of place for a human. Prisons are the new breeding grounds for gangs, which the government has easily classified as terrorism. A child can be swept up in this nonsensical craze, ultimately spending the rest of their life in prison, just for suspicion of being an "urban terrorist." Now, terms like mandatory minimum and NERA (No Early Release Act) become relevant. Once a child becomes a threat to society, his or her rights are irrelevant. They become a slave to involuntary servitude - prison!

Proper teaching from the mother and the father is the key. The 13th Amendment abolished slavery, except for under one condition - "Slavery shall remain appropriate as punishment for a crime."

Ruffin v. The Commonwealth is a landmark decision by the Virginia Supreme Court. The decision put to rest any notion that a convict is legally distinguishable from a slave - "For a time during his service in the penitentiary, he is in a state of penal servitude to the state. He, as a consequence of his crime, not only forfeits his liberty, but all his personal rights, except those which the law in its humanity accords to him. He is, for the time being, a slave of the state. He is civiliter mortuus; his estate, if he has any, is administered like that of a dead man."

S.T.O.P.! Let's not willingly raise our children where it is likely they will end up a slave! This advice is for parents who have seen the inside of a prison and those who have not. Those who have never been, don't go. Those who have been and have gotten out, don't ever go back. We need to be more intelligent with our decision making. And we need to teach our children to do the same.

We have to teach them that violence only begets violence. Shooting at a corrupt officer is not going to make him stop being corrupt. On the other hand, becoming a member of the force and reforming the department from within will change things and educate people at the same time. Don't hate the judge, lawyer, or prosecutor who railroaded you. Instead, join the legal profession so you can dictate the law in a fair and just manner. These are the ideologies that the youth must be taught. We have to teach them to take full advantage of their opportunities.

Push them to finish school. Take the civil exam. Join law enforcement. Hell, they could join the military. Direct them toward something that will give them the work ethic and discipline that they never learned in a single-parent home. Teach them that greatness is hard work. Greatness is an expense that is well worth the money. Anything of value, even things within the earth, must be dug for - gold, diamonds, oil... if you want it, you have to work for it.

Our people are no strangers to hard work. Most of us have our roots embedded in slavery. Young people don't really understand things like civil rights, Jim Crow laws, segregation or other occurrences in history that created the conditions we live in today. Slaves were kept ignorant and weren't allowed to read. Yet, in this day and age, we have the highest dropout rate of any nation. Slaves were killed if they even tried to educate themselves. Yet, today, we have young people who willingly underachieve when it comes to their education.

We have to teach them to get an associate's degree after they graduate high school. If they have an associate's degree, then teach them to get a bachelor's. If they have a bachelor's, then drive them toward getting a master's. The point is they must always harbor the desire to educate themselves. If the will to learn is strong, then the will to teach is even stronger.

Everyone needs a coach just like children need an adult who will not give up on them. The relationship between parents and children must be like teacher and student. S.T.O.P. by being a better teacher of the youth. Teach them through your actions. Intelligent people are more likely to make intelligent decisions. So let's take our youth and create a nation of intelligent minds.

10

Make Money Make Money

"A feast is made for laughter, and
wine makes life merry but money is
the answer for everything . . ."
- Ecclesiastes 10:19

Money, the pursuit of it or the things you buy with it, may not make you happy. It can, however, provide freedom of movement. Money can bring about ease and convenience. It can create possibilities that may solve many of life's dilemmas.

Having solutions to problems provides security. Having security allows you to focus on other matters so one can enjoy the nonmaterial aspects of life.

A newly released felon will have to learn legit ways of acquiring wealth. Most people live paycheck to paycheck without having anything saved for a rainy day. Many try to keep up with societal trends by living outside their means - the result of that is never good. If all a person has is $10,000, he or she should not spend $8,000 of it on a wedding just to make their spouse happy. A less expensive wedding is more rational for everyone involved. Another example is for a person to rent an apartment, but at the same time, they are paying a car note for a Benz or BMW. That money could be used to pay a mortgage on a house, a house which will one day become an asset.

Instead of living for the future, many of us live for the now. This causes a person to compete with his or her surroundings. Since so and so bought a Benz, so and so has to buy a Bentley, even if so and so can't afford it. With the expensive ride comes the need to have the clothes to match. People love looking like a million bucks, but don't know how to acquire a million bucks.

Achieving wealth is about sacrifice. Some may be born into their riches, others are going to have to put in that hard work. I remember watching the Steve Harvey Show when he said, "Inch by inch, anything is a cinch." I find these words especially true when it comes to saving and investing. Imagine saving $400 a month for five short years; $24,000 will have been amassed. This is $24,000 a person can simply play with, all because of saving little by little. All these bank deposits within five years gives you stability and dependability in the eyes of the banks. Now, acquiring loans or mortgages becomes a whole lot easier. Because this $24,000 was saved so easily and steadily, a bank will have no problem tripling this amount as a loan. The original $400 that was being saved per month can be used to make payments on the new loan, which should be paid within ten years. With consistent saving habits, the loan can be paid back sooner than that.

Okay, so there is $72,000 to spend, but let's not get foolish. The spending should respect the rules of the market. What is recession proof? What is in demand? One thing to answer both of these questions is property. Property will always be necessary. Even when the real estate market is not jumping, people are still looking to rent houses to alleviate the cost of owning property. This is when the business of land lording becomes beneficial. $50,000 of the $72,000 could be used as a down payment on a house. If the house costs around $100,000, essentially half the price will be paid, which means the mortgage will be extremely low. The house is in great condition. It's in a good neighborhood with good schools and decent people. Now a person will be willing to rent the property for top dollar. The owner is still paying a cheap rent, and the new house he is renting to someone else is helping him do that. The house has become a $50,000 investment that is paying back itself.

The house has an attic. A garage. A basement. Two baths. Three bedrooms. It's fenced in nicely with a groomed yard. It can easily - easily - be rented out for $1,600 a month. Keeping in mind the mortgage was only $500, maybe even less. This leaves $1,100, minus $400 for the bank loan, in a person's pockets.

After the down payment for the house, $22,000 remain. Within five years, this money and portions of other savings can be amassed to repeat the process. This time, a person is using his or her own money to purchase a house, and not a loan from a bank. Now there are two properties bringing in $1,600 a month. Due to the absence of a bank loan, the owner gets to pocket more money this go around.

Years later, after consistent savings and careful spending, a person is with their desired spouse, living the dream of any forty-year-old. Without bank loans. Financial independence. This is a luxury that will allow a person to go into business for themselves. Franchising a McDonalds, opening a beauty salon for both men and women - food and cosmetology are two things that will never go out of style. A thrifty dollar store is also an excellent business venture. This is because people still need to spend money when a recession hits. And what better place to spend money than a place where things of necessity cost only a dollar? In any event, all these decisions ensure that money will be making money.

Now ideas such as success on Wall Street become possible. A person could now research Warren Buffett or subscribe to the Wall Street Journal. The message is to accumulate assets and avoid liabilities. Be in a position to always have money coming in instead having to always push money out. No need for government assistance. No more living from check to check or from month to month. Comfort and security are now provided by sheer entrepreneurship.

Making money make money is important, but money truly isn't everything. It's really about the legacy a person wants to leave behind. S.T.O.P. is about putting others first. It's about getting away from the self-centered way of living we all used to adopt. Our success should trickle upon our loved ones. Our kids should have developed the same work ethic we had demonstrated. The generations to follow should have a fool-proof blueprint, a blueprint that can amass wealth that can remain in the family, then ultimately benefit the rest of the community.

Allowing our children to start out with a care package leaves little room for bad decision making. Some of our kids will still make the wrong choices, but the family will be in a better position to deal with the repercussions. Welfare will decrease. Recidivism will take a back slide. Mainly, because the need to commit crime will have decreased.   The thought of crimes is removed because people are focusing their efforts on making money make money.

Poverty will no longer be a reason to commit crime. Despair and depression will decrease dramatically. It's not the government's job to make these things happen - if it was, they would be doing it already. It's the parent's job to lie out the safety net for the youth. It's the parent's job to teach them that seasons may change, but skill sets will not. People will always need their snow shoveled in the winter, their leaves raked in the fall, and their grass cut in the spring and summer.

Kids need to learn that washing cars can lead to owning a car wash. Cutting grass can create the know-how for running a landscaping business. I remember a lady that lived in my neighborhood. She used to sell cups of flavored ice. $.25 cups to $2.00 cups. Those little pennies and dollars made money turn into more money. This lady understood the importance of making the right investment. Let's start thinking outside of prison by understanding how to use our creativity to generate wealth for the future of our children and their children's children.

About The Author

Jermaine Ali Williams is serving a lengthy sentence inside the New Jersey State Prison. While incarcerated, he realized that the world had gone off track. He reached within himself to deliver a message saying that everyone just needs to S.T.O.P.!

He used his prison stint to gain a high school diploma, as well as graduating from Blackstone Career Institute in Paralegal Studies. Williams also completed over a dozen therapeutic courses. His message is for the common man, rich man, gangster, politician, and all the classes from lower to upper – Know better and intend to do better. Start Thinking Outside Prison.

"Education is our passport to the future, for tomorrow belongs to the people who prepare for it today… " Malcom X

Thanks for your interest in
Freebird Publishers!

We value our customers and would love to hear from you! Reviews are an important part in bringing you quality publications. We love hearing from our readers-rather it's good or bad (though we strive for the best)!

If you could take the time to review/rate any publication you've purchased with Freebird Publishers we would appreciate it!

If your loved one uses Amazon, have them post your review on the books you've read. This will help us tremendously, in providing future publications that are even more useful to our readers and growing our business.

Amazon works off of a 5 star rating system. When having your loved one rate us be sure to give them your chosen star number as well as a written review. Though written reviews aren't required, we truly appreciate hearing from you.

☆ ☆ ☆ ☆ ☆ **Everything a prisoner needs is available in this book.**
January 30, 201 June 7, 2018
Format: Paperback

A necessary reference book for anyone in prison today. This book has everything an inmate needs to keep in touch with the outside world on their own from inside their prison cell. Inmate Shopper's business directory provides complete contact information on hundreds of resources for inmate services and rates the companies listed too! The book has even more to offer, contains numerous sections that have everything from educational, criminal justice, reentry, LGBT, entertainment, sports schedules and more. The best thing is each issue has all new content and updates to keep the inmate informed on todays changes. We recommend everybody that knows anyone in prison to send them a copy, they will thank you.

* No purchase neccessary. Reviews are not required for drawing entry. Void where prohibited.
  Contest date runs July 1 - June 30, 2019.

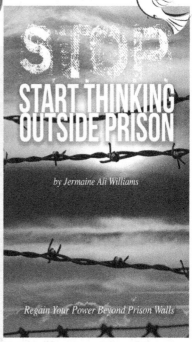

PENACON

Penacon is owned and operated by Freebird Publishers, your trusted inmate service provider.

Penacon.com dedicated to assisting the imprisoned community find connections of friendship and romance around the world. Your profile will be listed on our user-friendly website. We make sure yo profile is seen at the highest visibility rate available by driving traffic to our site by consistent adverti and networking. We know how important it is to have your ad seen by as many people as possible in order to bring you the best service possible. Pen pals can now email their first message through penacon.com! We print and send these messages with return addresses if you get one. We value yo business and process profiles promptly.

To receive your informational package and application send two stamps to:

PENACON

Box 533
North Dighton, MA 02764
Penacon@freebirdpublishers.com
Corrlinks: diane@freebirdpublishers.com
JPay: diane@freebirdpublishers.com

Freebird Publishers

Presents A New Self-Help Reentry Book

NEW RULES FOR A NEW YOU

Things don't magically change after you get kicked out of prison. Life starts all over again but there's a catch, having a record impacts almost every part of your life. With this book you'll find out how to prepare for life as an ex-offender. Filled with insights, advice, contacts, and exercises the information strikes legal, personal and professional levels. A real world guide for minimizing disruptions and maximizing success.

Life With A Record helps make sense of the major challenges facing ex-offenders today. Ten hard hitting chapters outline the purpose of making a Strategic Reentry Plan and making peace with supervisors, family, your community and your future. Written by well-known reentry technician Anthony Tinsman, it packs an amazing amount of material into its pages and gives you a quick, easy to follow, full spectrum of instruction.

Inside You Will Find:

☑ How to rebuild your credit and begin financial recovery

☑ Halfway house rules and supervision terms

☑ Special grants and loans to finance education, job training, or starting a business

☑ Legal tips for dealing with discrimination in employment, housing and collegiate settings

☑ Discussion of success stories, best practices, reuniting families, plus much more

☑ Directory with hundreds of reentry contacts

☑ Sample forms and documents that cut through red tape

☑ How to regain your civil and political rights

Life With a Record explores the most commonly confronted issues and attitudes that sabotage reentry. It provides tools that cut across functions of discrimination, in corporations, political life and throughout society. It opens the door to empowerment, reminding ex-offenders that change and long term freedom begins with a commitment to daily growth. Addressing the whole reentry process, Life With a Record is "must" reading for anyone preparing to leave prison and face the world. It's an ideal book for ex-offenders with decades of experience as well as first time prisoners who need help jump starting their new life.

INSIDE COMPLETE REENTRY RESOURCE LISTINGS

Hundreds of complete, up-to-date entries at your fingertips.

Life With A Record

Only $25.99

Plus $7 S/H with tracking

Softcover, 8" x 10", B&W, 360 pages

NO ORDER FORM NEEDED CLEARLY WRITE ON PAPER & SEND PAYMENT TO:

Freebird Publishers Box 541, North Dighton, MA 02764

Diane@FreebirdPublishers.com www.FreebirdPublishers.com

Toll Free: 888-712-1987 Text/Phone: 774-406-8682

MoneyGram.

Made in United States
Orlando, FL
18 February 2022

14955594R00046